Problem Regions of Europe

General Editor: **D. I. Scargill**

North Rhine–Westphalia
J. A. Hellen

Oxford University Press

Oxford University Press, Ely House, London W.1

OXFORD LONDON GLASGOW NEW YORK
TORONTO MELBOURNE WELLINGTON CAPE TOWN
IBADAN NAIROBI DAR ES SALAAM LUSAKA ADDIS ABABA
KUALA LUMPUR SINGAPORE JAKARTA HONG KONG TOKYO
DELHI BOMBAY CALCUTTA MADRAS KARACHI

© Oxford University Press 1974

First published 1974
Second impression 1976

I should like, above all, to record my gratitude to
Dr. Kurt and Dr. Dorothea Schlacht. I am also most
grateful for the unfailing helpfulness and generosity
of all the official bodies, industrial concerns, and
individuals who have facilitated the preparation of this
volume. Special thanks are due to a number of
ministries in Düsseldorf, to the Siedlungsverband
Ruhrkohlenbezirk, and to the city administration of
Gelsenkirchen.

The University of Newcastle upon Tyne provided
financial support for fieldwork in 1972, and this is
gratefully acknowledged.

J. A. H.

Filmset by BAS Printers Limited, Wallop, Hampshire
and printed in Great Britain
at the University Press, Oxford
by Vivian Ridler, Printer to the University

Editor's Preface

Great economic and social changes have taken place in Europe in recent years. The agricultural workforce in the west was halved, for example, during the 1950s and 1960s. This unprecedented flight from the land has made possible some much-needed reorganization of farm holdings but it has also created problems, not least that of finding uses for land in the highlands and elsewhere where it is no longer profitable to farm. Closely related is the difficulty of maintaining services to a much diminished rural population or of providing new kinds of services for the holidaymakers who increasingly buy up rural properties.

Contraction of the labour force has also taken place in many traditional industries. The coal-mining industry alone has shed two-thirds of its workforce since 1950. The resulting problems have been especially serious in those mining or manufacturing districts which have a high level of dependence on a single source of employment—a not uncommon result of Europe's industrial past—and the efforts of those who seek to attract new industries are often thwarted by a legacy of pollution, bad housing, and soured labour relations.

Quite a different set of problems has arisen in the great cities of Europe such as London and Paris and in the conurbations of closely linked cities well exemplified by Randstad Holland. Here are problems due to growth brought about by the expansion of consumer-orientated manufacturing and still more by the massive increase in office jobs which proliferate in 'down-town' business districts. The problems are economic, social and political, and they include the effects of congestion, of soaring land values, of the increasing divorce of place of residence from place of work, and of the difficulty of planning a metropolitan region that may be shared between many independent-minded local authorities.

The problems resulting from change are not passing ones; indeed they exhibit a persistence that amply justifies their study on an areal basis. Hence the *Problem Regions of Europe* series. The volumes in the series have all been written by geographers who, by the nature of their discipline, can take a broadly based approach to description and analysis. Geographers in the past have been reluctant to base their studies on problem regions since the problem was often of a temporary nature, less enduring than the 'personality' of the region, but the magnitude of present-day problems has even resulted in the suggestion that regions should be defined in terms of the problems that confront them.

Certain themes emerge clearly when the basis of the problem is examined: the effects of a harsh environment, of remoteness, and of political division, as well as of industrial decay or urban congestion. But these have not been examined in isolation and the studies that make up the series have been carefully chosen in order that useful comparisons can be made. Thus, for example, both the Mezzogiorno and Andalusia have to contend with the problems of Mediterranean drought, wind, and flood, but the precise nature of these and other problems, as well as man's response to them, differs in the two regions. Similarly, the response to economic change is not the same in North-East England as in North Rhine-Westphalia, nor the response to social pressures the same in Paris as in the Randstad.

The efforts which individual governments have made to grapple with their problems provides a basis for critical assessment in each of the volumes. For too long solutions were sought that were piecemeal and short-term. Our own Development Areas in Britain provide a good illustration of this kind of policy. Of late, however, European governments have shown an increasing awareness of the need to undertake planning on a regional basis. The success or otherwise of such regional policies is fully explored in the individual *Problem Region* volumes.

When it was first planned the *Problem Region* series was thought of merely as useful to the sixth-form student of geography. As it has developed it has become clear that the authors— all specialists in the geography of the areas concerned—have contributed studies that will be useful, not only for sixth-form work, but as a basis for the more detailed investigations undertaken by advanced students, both of geography and of European studies in general.

D.I.S.

St. Edmund Hall
August 1973

Contents

Introduction

Problems in other countries, like failings in other people, are usually more easily recognized than understood by the outsider. Few areas of the globe can have faced problems more severe and heterogeneous than those of North Rhine–Westphalia, West Germany's most important and populous *Land* located at the centre of the 'Golden Triangle' linking London, Hamburg, and Paris; yet probably no other comparable area has generated so much intelligent self-examination and self-criticism amongst its inhabitants. Likewise probably no comparable area has produced such a mass of literary, statistical, and cartographic documentation on the whole and the parts of its region. Outside Germany some of the problems to be discussed in this book are well known in outline—the post-war reconstruction programme and the more recent decline of the fortunes of the Ruhr coal industry are two examples—but the lessons to be drawn from the problems and their solutions have not been so widely examined.

Many of the problems are unique to the German context and must be seen in terms of culture and history no less than in the circumstances of the extraordinarily rapid and complex innovation and change powered by West Germany's post-war affluence. They are more typically problems of over-development rather than of under-development. Other problems, however, are already shared in general outline, if not in particular detail, by similar technologically advanced urban-based societies, and it is the peculiarly German approach in evaluating and solving problems which is so interesting in comparative studies of European problem regions. The outmoded reputation which still clings to the Ruhr of popular imagination is just one example of how images change much more slowly than reality. Regions may indeed define themselves in terms of the problems with which they are confronted and it is the geographer who, despite the deceptive simplicity of his art, reflects the rate and extent to which man is transforming the earth. Geographical space may, by comparison with the abstract and topological dimensions of organizational space, appear to be the less subtle, but the real landscape is often the outward expression of deep-seated and complexly interacting processes, as well as being the datum point from which to measure change or to establish continuity from the past, and it repays study.

All problems can of course be variously defined as issues involving difficulty, uncertainty, doubt, or ambiguity. When applied to some geographical area or environmental context they may in addition be either actual or potential problems, and hence be diagnosable or predictable. The German term *Problemkreis* offers a valuable conceptual approach when discussing problems or problem regions, if only because it reminds one that in the reality of place most problems are interlocked with others, and that to isolate one or more factors is often to distort interpretation. Faced with the task of relating problems to regions the geographer may choose between two distinctive approaches to his information: either he can analyse spatial patterns or he can systematically trace the chronological development of his subject. North Rhine–Westphalia experiences a range of problems in its relationships to larger units no less than amongst its constituent parts, and the sub-regional linkages in particular offer a productive field for inquiry. Whether the problems arise from North Rhine–Westphalia's relationships with the Federal Republic or the E.E.C., for example, or from internal disequilibrium between one town and the next, they commonly arise because adaptation to change and growth is far from uniform. Conventionally the geographer may speak of environmental, locational, social or economic problem categories, which lend themselves to comparative study. But in the context of the massive scale of contemporary planned change and intervention, it may be useful to divide problems into three *time* categories first, and only then examine selected examples in their regional setting. Conceived of in this way, problems fall into three classes:

(1) Legacies from the past—a group which may include the inherent features of a region's physical environment or geographical location no less than its historically conditioned circumstances.

(2) Contemporary problems—these may be anticipated or quite unforeseen, and they may result from actions, changes, or decisions taken inside or outside the affected region.

(3) Potential or prospective problems—a group

which may be predicted by extrapolating from contemporary circumstances, or which are contingent upon the 'blueprints' of politicians, planners or industrialists who seek to determine the future of society and economy.

It probably bears re-stating that problems are an integral part of most modern social and economic change, and that all regions experiencing change are in this sense problem regions. North Rhine–Westphalia is uncommon, however, in being faced simultaneously by problems of the past, the present, and the future, at a level of complexity which provides few precedents and

even fewer guidelines. The particular choice of area is justified by the overriding importance of the German State (*Land*) as an administrative, functional, and planning unit. As with other titles in this series, adjustment to change will be the major theme for discussion. Problems of industrial decay, of urban congestion, of over-development could each scarcely be other than central in any treatment of North Rhine–Westphalia, but the reader's attention will be deliberately directed to causes and effects which are shown to reach far beyond the specific sub-regions or sectors with which they are normally associated.

Fig. 1. North Rhine-Westphalia: natural regions

1 North Rhine-Westphalia in the European Context

Although larger in size than neighbouring Belgium, North Rhine–Westphalia* with an area of 34 054 square kilometres is territorially only the fourth largest of the Federal German *Länder* (States). But with a population over 17 million, and one-third of the country's industrial turnover, it dominates the Republic as it dominated the Europe of the Six. Bonn, the provisional Federal Capital, lies near its southern border, but no primate city commands the *Land* or region like a Paris or a London. No less than 10 million people live in the Rhine-Ruhr agglomeration, and 13 cities have populations in excess of 200 000 in a group headed by Köln (Cologne) and including Essen, Düsseldorf, and Dortmund. The Rhine-Ruhr agglomeration alone accounted for 40·4 per cent of the Federal total in 1967; in addition NRW contains the four other smaller agglomerations of Aachen, Bielefeld-Herford, Siegen, and Münster. The importance of these areas in planning strategy will be discussed later, but at this stage it will be sufficient to note that the division into inner metropolitan, outer metropolitan, and rural areas is as fundamental to geographical understanding as it is to planning practice.

NRW's is a central position in an enlarged European Community. Indeed not only is it at the geographical centre but also it is central to its consumer market: within a radius of 150 km from Essen-Dortmund there live 30 million people, within 300 km 70 million, and within 500 km over 140 million. Not surprisingly, many of NRW's current problems centre on transportation—public and private, national and international—and the improvement of the transport infrastructure (whether road, rail, water, or pipeline) is radically altering existing patterns of settlement and economic geography.

The natural framework

The division of NRW into a number of natural regions is shown in Fig. 1, the importance of which will become evident in the discussion of numerous problems, chiefly environmental and locational. Without attempting here any explanation of the somewhat involved terminology of

*Hereafter referred to as NRW.

German 'landscape' geography, its importance in German geographical literature should be stressed. A hierarchy of landscape units or natural regions is commonly recognized, and these have been systematically mapped down to the smallest site or ecotope—a terrain inventory valuable as a planning framework and in such practical applications as agriculture, forestry, hydrology, and conservation. Here only the *Naturräume* are shown—each of which has a more or less characteristic assemblage of interrelated physical phenomena—together with the more important of their sub-regions.

The striking contrast is between the upland and lowland areas, the former mainly part of Hercynian Europe and the German Central Uplands, the latter a fringe belt of the North German Plain subtly affected by the Ice Age deposits and the vertical and horizontal movements of the proto-Rhine and other rivers. The altitudinal range is considerable in the rise from the dyked landscape near Kleve (12 m) to the exposed Kahler Asten (841 m) of the far southeastern Sauerland, and this three-dimensional aspect has obvious significance in climatic gradations.

The **Lower Rhine Plain** marks the transition from the margins of the former Rhine delta near the Dutch border to the highly fertile loess-covered bay south of Düsseldorf. Some 4613 km² in extent, the topography has been shaped not only by the shifting course and changing deposits of the Rhine itself but also by the events during and after the Ice Age when a series of river terraces formed and varied aeolian and other deposits were laid upon them. The Lower Rhine area is far from being a featureless plain, however. Now regulated, the river runs through an easily flooded alluvial zone, parallel to which is the similar landscape of the Niers, a tributary of the Maas, separated by a marked line of morainic hills, the Lower Rhine Heights.

The **Köln-Bonn (or Lower Rhine) Bay**, although smaller in extent (3487 km²) than the Lower Rhine Plain is far more important in the context of NRW. The region is well defined by its upland rim from the southern point near Bonn where it emerges from the Rhine Gorge. Beneath its surface lies a complex series of block faults, by far the most important feature of which is the Ville horst separating the Erft and Köln blocks to west and east respectively. Over a Devonian basement has been laid down a series of Tertiary marine and lacustrine deposits, chiefly alternating sands or clays and brown coal covering an area some 2500 km² in extent. As a result of the favourable interaction of climate and tectonics, brown coal beds of up to 105 m thickness have been preserved at workable depths.

At or near the surface, the Köln-Bonn Bay is further characterized by a well-marked sequence of river terraces—the high, main, middle, and low respectively—fairly easily identified by height (and land-use) in the field. These have been greatly modified by aeolian deposits ranging from coarse blown sands (*Flugsand*) to loess (*Löss*), plus subsequent re-sorting and the soil-forming processes. In particular the loess cover of the west gives rise to two highly fertile sub-regions, the *Börden* of Jülich and Zülpich, in which the loam is often 5 m deep.

The **Westphalian or Münster Bay** forms the third of the lowland areas, but with 10 013 km² it is far larger than the two former regions oriented to the Rhine. A large part does drain via the Lippe to the Rhine, but the Ems headwaters are important in the east. As a region the Münster Bay is clearly defined in the south and east by the uplands, but the lowland periphery is less clearly differentiated. The region includes much of the Ruhr District (strictly part of the Emscher-Land) and therefore extends over some Palaeozoic rocks, but in the main the Bay is floored by younger, particularly Cretaceous rocks such as chalk, sandstones, and marls. In the south, marked by the line of the ancient east to west trade route of the *Hellweg*, a fertile *Börde* landscape extends from the Haarstrang hills just north of the Ruhr-Möhne valleys practically to the Lippe. Northwards again the Westphalian Bay falls into three main sub-regions, the western and eastern parts of the Münsterland cohering round the Kern-Münsterland. This core is marked, in an area of light relief, by three hilly areas on its periphery—the Haltern Heights and Baumberg and Beckum Hills—whereas elsewhere in the Münsterland the principal distinctions away from the extensive terraces of the Ems valley arise from the varied distribution of Ice Age deposits.

The uplands, particularly those of the south, stand in marked contrast to these low-lying areas. The Eifel and Süderbergland separated by the Rhine may be grouped together as part of the Rhenish Uplands and in turn part of Hercynian Europe, whereas the Weser Hills form a distinctive

scarp and vale region of softer Mesozoic rocks.

Along the Belgian border the **Eifel** and **Venn** form only a small part of the great Ardennes-Eifel region, much of which extends south to the Moselle but outside NRW. This part of the Eifel forms mainly a deeply dissected plateau at up to 600 m, complex in its geology and structure and ranging across many rock types, particularly slates, some of which are mineralized with iron, lead, and zinc ores. The strike is characteristically from south-west to north-east and in an area of high rainfall such valleys as those of the Rur and Urft have provided important reservoir sites.

The **Süderbergland** is likewise an area of complex geology, which incorporates some of the oldest structural features and rocks in NRW. Conventionally it falls into a Rheno-Hercynian Zone in the south and high-faulted Westphalian Zone and Foreland in the North. Its largely Devonian rocks are chiefly of slate, sandstone, and quartzite, locally mineralized. The Ruhr Coal Basin, like the smaller coalfield around Aachen, lies along the northern edge of the Hercynian block where the Carboniferous rocks dip beneath younger measures.

With a total area of 8971 km², the Süderbergland falls into a number of highly distinctive sub-regions, marked by their south-west to north-east strike, of which the Bergisches Land, the Siegerland and the Sauerland are the dominant components. As with the Eifel, so in these uplands the high rainfall and the drainage network of rivers such as the Ruhr and Sieg are important factors in water supply to the industrialized lowlands. Generally poor upland soils account for a farming pattern quite unlike that of the lowlands, and the extensive forest cover serves further to bring out the physical contrasts.

The **Weser Hills** form the third upland region, albeit much more modest in altitude and quite unlike the hills on either side of the Rhine. The northern section (lower Weserbergland) some 2671 km² in extent is well defined by two hill ranges, the scarps of the Osning contiguous with the Münsterland, and in the north-east the Wiehen Hills; between them lies a hilly but less resistant landscape of Keuper marls and Liassic clay slates popularly called the Ravensberger Land and Lipper Land and other Triassic or Jurassic rocks. Further south the line of the Osning is continued by the Egge Hills, west of which lies the important limestone Paderborn Plateau and east of which the much hillier upper Weserbergland (3757 km²). The Weser river flows mainly outside NRW, but where it breaches

Reg. Präs. Nord Wüttemberg, Stuttgart No.38.684

Hilchenbach, an isolated resort in the Rothaargebirge of the Siegerland. Provision of water, forestry products, and recreational facilities by areas such as this reflects the complementary functions of upland and lowland.

the Wiehen Hills at the Porta Westfalica it has created a highly important routeway linking Westphalia and the Rhine with northern Germany.

The man-made framework

Surveying the face of NRW today it is difficult to appreciate that for most Germans, May 1945 was the 'darkest hour'. The country had capitulated, the lower Rhine and the Ruhr presented a landscape of catastrophe, a *Ruinenstaat*, industry and agriculture had been brought to a virtual standstill, and a flood of refugees was surging westwards. North Rhine–Westphalia had undergone total war to a degree unparalleled in Germany save for Hamburg and Bremen. Not only had massive air-raids, particularly in 1944, sought to annihilate Ruhr industry; the western borders had been bitterly fought over as the Allies marched on the Rhine. Small towns like Jülich (97 per cent destroyed) and Emmerich (91 per cent) had been virtually obliterated, whilst great cities like Dortmund and Köln (over 60 per cent) and Bochum and Essen (over 50 per cent) were

in ruins. One is reminded of a somewhat paradoxical if macabre advertisement in a British newspaper: over a selection of photographs of ruined cities and plant, many of them in NRW, ran the caption 'By 1945, Germany had won a huge industrial advantage'.

The modern NRW came into existence as an administrative unit with the amalgamation of the former provinces of Nordrhein and Westfalen by the British occupation forces on 18 July 1946. (The Lippe-Detmold area was added in January 1947.) Before 1871 the Rhineland in particular had been split into numerous political sub-units; in that year both the Rhineland and Westphalia had become Prussian provinces at a time when the *Rheinisch-Westfälische Industriegebiet* was moving towards a phase of massive development. In broad outline this division persisted until 1945. Most of the changes to be discussed are compressed into the comparatively short period since 1946, when the reconstruction of NRW began. But before developing particular themes it will be helpful to outline the administrative framework on which so many statistical sources

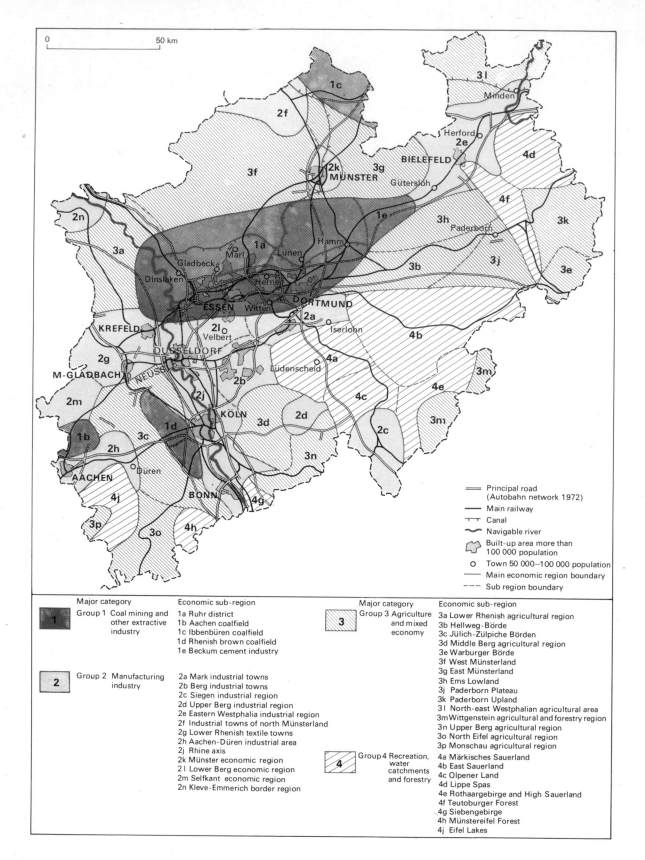

	Major category	Economic sub-region
1	Group 1 Coal mining and other extractive industry	1a Ruhr district 1b Aachen coalfield 1c Ibbenbüren coalfield 1d Rhenish brown coalfield 1e Beckum cement industry
2	Group 2 Manufacturing industry	2a Mark industrial towns 2b Berg industrial towns 2c Siegen industrial region 2d Upper Berg industrial region 2e Eastern Westphalia industrial region 2f Industrial towns of north Münsterland 2g Lower Rhenish textile towns 2h Aachen-Düren industrial area 2j Rhine axis 2k Münster economic region 2l Lower Berg economic region 2m Selfkant economic region 2n Kleve-Emmerich border region

	Major category	Economic sub-region
3	Group 3 Agriculture and mixed economy	3a Lower Rhenish agricultural region 3b Hellweg-Börde 3c Jülich-Zülpiche Börden 3d Middle Berg agricultural region 3e Warburger Börde 3f West Münsterland 3g East Münsterland 3h Ems Lowland 3j Paderborn Plateau 3k Paderborn Upland 3l North-east Westphalian agricultural area 3m Wittgenstein agricultural and forestry region 3n Upper Berg agricultural region 3o North Eifel agricultural region 3p Monschau agricultural region
4	Group 4 Recreation, water catchments and forestry	4a Märkisches Sauerland 4b East Sauerland 4c Olpener Land 4d Lippe Spas 4e Rothaargebirge and High Sauerland 4f Teutoburger Forest 4g Siebengebirge 4h Münstereifel Forest 4j Eifel Lakes

Legend:
— Principal road (Autobahn network 1972)
— Main railway
⊤ Canal
∿ Navigable river
Built-up area more than 100 000 population
○ Town 50 000–100 000 population
— Main economic region boundary
-- Sub region boundary

TABLE I
Administrative areas 1971

Regierungsbezirk	Area (km²)	Gemeinden	Landkreise	Cities	Population (thousands)
Düsseldorf	5505	143	9	13	5667
Köln	4004	86	6	2	2462
Aachen	3098	177	7	1	1029
Münster	7209	174	10	6	2424
Detmold	6491	331	12	1	1761
Arnsberg	7746	332	12	11	3746

are based, as well as the main features of NRW's economy.

Administration

Since 1972, when Aachen was absorbed into Köln, NRW has been divided into five middle-tier units or *Regierungsbezirke* and further sub-divided into 56 *Kreise* (administrative districts) and 34 *Kreisfreie Städte* or independent cities. The basic constitution guarantees the autonomy of *Gemeinden* or local authorities, which since 1808 have been the smallest administrative units. Progressively over recent years the number of *Gemeinden* has been reduced, however, as part of local government reform, and from a figure of 2365 in 1961 the total had fallen to 984 by 1973.

Economic regions

The regions portrayed in Fig. 2 are intended only as a generalized indication of the dominant economic activities in various parts of NRW. Broadly four categories are recognized:

(1) Areas dominated by coal mining and/or large-scale industry.

(2) The major regions of manufacturing industry, often with marked local specialization.

(3) Regions dominated by agricultural activities but with variable degrees of industrial activity, particularly in the towns.

(4) The upland areas characterized by their importance in forestry and recreation and as water catchments.

The situation schematically presented here is far from static. In many ways such a map helps to identify problems associated with unbalanced economic and social structures inherited from regional specializations forged in the past. Present-day inequalities of opportunity are less easily discerned in a region which not only has full employment but also gives work to over 500 000 foreign workers in a workforce of 6·5 million. But the rate and direction of change becomes obvious when patterns of internal migration, of commuting, and of employment structure and growth rates by sector are examined district by district.

Fig. 2. Economic regions (schematic) *Source: S.V.R. Regionalplanung (Atlas) 1960*

2 Legacies from the Past

Agriculture and rural societies

As in most highly developed countries, so in NRW the agricultural sector poses many problems of adjustment to change. Living standards and expectations have risen in an unprecedented way for most of the population not working on the land, whereas the peasantry in particular have become an underprivileged class in this, the most densely populated *Land* (average 507 inhabitants per km² or 297 per km² in the rural districts). Changing markets, technical innovation, and agricultural policies remotely decided in Brussels or Bonn have all compounded the strains on a rural society facing erosion not only of a traditional life-style but also of its workforce. In an economy in which industrial growth outstrips population, the rural areas have become pools of potential labour and the raising of productivity and money income has become for many a key to the survival of traditional farming.

For the geographer the morphology of the rural landscape paints a deceptively clear picture of an archaic society and agrarian structure. The rural settlements and individual farmsteads, no less than the mosaic of unhedged fields, have a timelessness about them. Superficially it is true to say that German agriculture in general is inefficient in terms of land, labour, and capital— although in this regard NRW suffers less than most of the *Länder*—but closer study of the history and sociology of rural communities, or of the individual farmer's response to change, shows how easily the outsider can be misled. The 'timeless' aura of peasant farming is more often an indication of continuity and a capacity for survival than of an archaic existence.

Soil resources

Mining apart, agriculture tends to show the clearest links between natural conditions and resource exploitation. The average farm size is shown in Fig. 3, and the soil quality is represented by five classes, differentiated numerically on a scale from 0 to 100. (The original sheets were mapped for taxation purposes from 1934, taking the best soils in Germany as 100; they are particularly valuable as an inventory of land potential in questions of competing land-use and in planning land apportionment.) The best soil class in NRW occurs exclusively in the fertile,

deep loessial soils of the Köln Bay, whilst the very good soils (mainly loess-loam) are more widely spread in the Rhineland, the Soester *Börde* and the Weser Hills. Contrasting with these is the wide extent of classes IV and V, a group which includes not only the acid upland soils largely derived from weathered slate, but also those of the sandy heathlands (*Senne*) or waterlogged moorlands (*Moore*) of the lowlands. Climate exerts more immediate effects with altitude, the onset of the growing season for example varying by as much as five to six weeks between favoured lowland farms and the high Sauerland, and arable farming is usually uneconomic above 400 m. Very generally the contrast in farming regions is that between wheat, vegetables, sugar beet, potatoes, pigs, and dairying in the lowlands, and rye, oats, permanent grass, and beef cattle in the uplands, where forestry,

TABLE 2
Land-use 1971

	Area (km²)	%
Agricultural land	1 922 856	56·4
Fallow land★	28 552	0·8
Forests, woodland	808 289	23·7
Uncultivated moorland, wasteland, etc.	71 397	2·1
Built-up land	271 477	8·0
Roads, railways, etc.	189 785	5·6
Water surfaces	50 716	1·5
Parks, sports areas, etc.	66 870	2·0
Total area	3 409 942	

★Fallow land here signifies unused agricultural land rather than 'resting'.

sometimes linked with farming, is highly important. The overall land-use in 1971 is shown in Table 2; of particular interest is the inexorable pressure of competition for land from expanding urban settlements and communications networks.

The peasantry

Peasant society cannot be dismissed convincingly in a few lines. The overall importance of the group can be gauged from the fact that of 162 610 agricultural holdings (with some 250 000 full-time workers) in 1971, only 3204 came into the

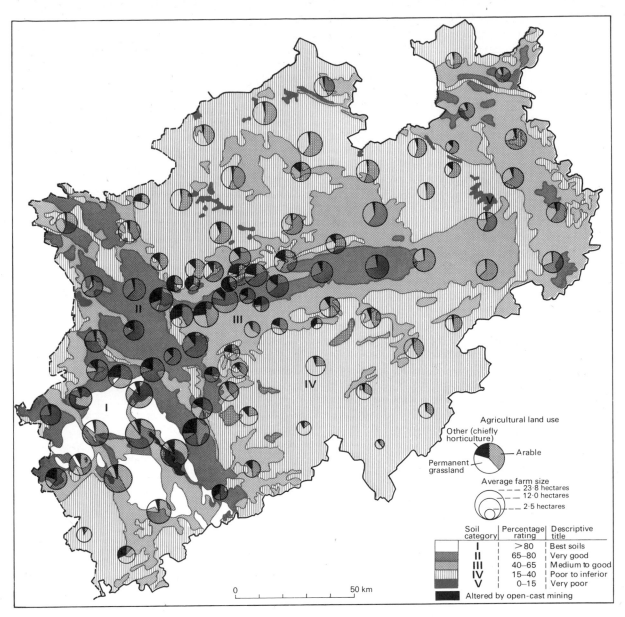

Agricultural land use

Other (chiefly horticulture) — Arable
Permanent grassland

Average farm size
23·8 hectares
12·0 hectares
2·5 hectares

Soil category	Percentage rating	Descriptive title
I	>80	Best soils
II	65–80	Very good
III	40–65	Medium to good
IV	15–40	Poor to inferior
V	0–15	Very poor
		Altered by open-cast mining

0   50 km

Fig. 3. Soil quality and farm size

non-peasant class of capitalist farm above 50 hectares, and only a further 26 853 holdings could qualify as 'large' peasant farms (20–50 ha). Basic to the peasantry is the family farm, characterized by its self-sufficiency, as much social as economic. The peasant is born into the *Bauernstand*; into a definite estate, rather than a class, in the historical sense of the term. Many of the everyday words associated with the rural environment have, importantly, both a spatial and a social connotation, linking the contemporary peasant with a feudal and, more remotely, tribal past. His forebears fought for their rights in the Peasant Wars of the fifteenth and sixteenth centuries and, like the nobility, they have been, to quote Pfeifer, 'forces for stability, contrasted with the forces for mobility of the third and fourth estates (*Bürgertum* and *Arbeitertum*)'. Today this stability is at a discount in the modern state and the move from traditional farming to 'agribusiness' is squeezing many marginal farmers out of existence. The obsolescence of the peasantry is largely due to its historical legacy, particularly to the tenacious ownership, as opposed to tenancy, of small and unviable units and the stubbornly inefficient use of labour and capital in an attempt to increase output at the expense of productivity.

It is unwise to generalize about peasant farming, however, and certain cultural distinctions within NRW should be emphasized. The settlement pattern as such shows great variations; in the Münsterland for example, dispersed farms became separated from the original medieval villages (generally *Haufendörfer*), whereas in parts of the south closed villages grew out of a primary dispersed settlement (*Einzelhöfe*). As the more fertile areas were settled, so over the centuries the waste-land and forest were colonized. The major cultural distinction is between the western Frankish zone, roughly south of Düsseldorf and Wuppertal, and the larger Saxon zone in the north and east, the persistence of which is typified by the distinctiveness of the clustered Frankish farmstead contrasting with the unitary Saxon farmhouse in which animals, implements, harvested crops, and the farming family are sheltered beneath a single roof. Many of today's problems may be attributed to the decline of traditional economies associated with these settlement and house types, and to the systems of inheritance—particularly of equally divided inheritance expressed in outmoded field shapes and sizes.

Today the most striking feature of change is the reduction in the number of holdings and the fall in the full-time agricultural workforce. The relative decline in importance of agriculture in the total workforce has persisted for nearly a century, but the post-war restructuring of agriculture heralds an absolute change. Fig. 3 is helpful in linking the rural past with the present, emphasizing as it does the small average size of holdings on a *Kreis* basis—overall 10·9 ha in 1971 —and the regional concentration of the most marginal of these in the north-east or along the southern margins of NRW. Table 3 confirms the changes which have occurred in different size-classes between 1949 and 1971, particularly as a result of the progressive rise in the threshold-size for economically viable farm units. Immediately after the war when the food ration fell to no more than 900 calories a day, the farming sector held the key to survival; production actually declined between 1945 and 1948. Today about half of the NRW's food consumption can be satisfied from internal sources, but within a generation the peasant has witnessed a swing from the crisis of food deficit (in which self-sufficiency made the peasant a vital worker), to a crisis of agricultural surplus (in which a Common Agricultural Policy seeks, at the expense of the same small farmer, to 'harmonize' a sluggish demand with rapid improvements in technology and productivity).

Although cropping and livestock patterns have changed considerably, monetary returns in relation to farm size and labour inputs are decisive in assessing the impact of voluntary adjustments by the peasants and the intervention of the official *Agrarpolitik*. Thus between 1949 and 1971 the number of units in NRW fell by 40 per cent overall. Holdings in the 20 to 50 ha class rose by 41 per cent over that period, and there was a more modest 21 per cent increase in the holdings over 50 ha. During 1968, farms at the critical size of 20 ha and above for the first time accounted for just over half the land under agriculture in NRW. Many of the smallest (0·5 to 2·0 ha) are highly specialized and intensively worked as market gardens and nurseries or as part-time concerns, but the next size-classes (2·1 to 5 and

TABLE 3A
NRW : Changes in size and number of agricultural holdings 1949–60

Class (by size of holding)	1949				1960			
	Number	%	Total area (ha)	%	Number	%	Total area (ha)	%
0·01–2 ha	104 078	38·9	103 924	5·5	72 878	33·8	72 201	3·9
2·1–5 ha	61 847	23·2	200 556	10·7	44 216	20·6	144 612	7·8
5·1–10 ha	44 716	16·7	321 225	17·0	36 373	16·9	266 283	14·5
10·1–20 ha	35 124	13·1	491 768	26·1	37 964	17·7	537 197	29·2
20·1–50 ha	19 015	7·1	553 345	29·4	20 841	9·7	606 502	33·0
50·1 ha and over	2 648	1·0	213 644	11·3	2 724	1·3	213 280	11·6
Totals	267 428	100	1 884 462	100	214 996	100	1 840 075	100

5·1 to 10 ha), the marginal peasant farms, have come under increasing pressure, and now account for only 14·1 per cent of the total area, a mere one-half of their 1949 extent. This decline has continued and sends shock-waves into the high size-classes as productivity demands greater and greater economies of scale, and even medium-scale peasants find it increasingly hard to earn a 'living wage'. It should, however, be noted that much of the transfer from smaller to larger holdings is by leasehold rather than outright sale: the overall ratio of ownership to tenancy of land is roughly 70 : 30.

In keeping with this process of amalgamations and concentration of production, the workforce has shown a similar marked decline in numbers. In Germany as a whole, around 10 per cent of the workforce was engaged in agriculture in 1971, but for NRW the figure was nearer 4 per cent; by 1980 it is hoped to reduce this Federal proportion to 5·6 per cent, thereby freeing 1 million workers for relocation. In the ten years from 1956 to 1966 the total number of those employed in agriculture on holdings of over 2 ha in NWR fell by 31 per cent from 622 000 to 431 000. By 1970 the number was 364 000. Where the hired labour force had totalled 151 000 in 1956, by 1970 it had fallen to a mere 34 000. Family labour had fallen much more slowly, but whereas the number of full-time workers had declined sharply, the part-time element showed little change over the period. Some of these changes are undoubtedly attributable to better wages and conditions obtainable by leaving the land, but mechanization on the one hand and government incentives on the other have all been important in transforming an apparently permanent feature of German society and rural landscape. Whatever the causes of redeployment, one of the crucial improvements has been in raised labour productivity; in the broad spectrum of farming conditions and specialisms, generalization is misleading, but the NRW average employment ratio of one full-time worker per 7 ha of farmland has obvious implications for the many family farms which have less land per head than this.

Changes in crops and livestock

Many problems of adjustment are reflected in changes in crop acreages and livestock numbers. In particular the farmer in NRW faces not only competition from within the country but also that of other E.E.C. producers. Over the post-war period there has been a general increase in crop yields, but the productivity gains from mechanization depend on field shape and size; similarly the move towards growing only crops that can be cultivated and harvested by machine— horticulture being an obvious exception—tends to favour areas with friable soils. Wholesale price movements over the period 1964 to 1971 confirm the smaller farmers' marketing difficulties: all grains, flour, potatoes, beef, pork, and butter were lower in price by the close of the period, although the farm-worker's wage had risen by about 50 per cent in that time.

A graph for the last twenty years would show a massive relative decline for most individual crops (particularly potatoes, fodder crops, rye, and oats) with only barley, sugar beet, and wheat showing advances. Whereas in 1950 nearly 56 per cent of the arable land was under grain crops and 14·2 per cent under potatoes, by 1971 these figures were 76·8 per cent and 1·9 per cent respectively. In the vegetable sector competition from other E.E.C. regions has led to a change from coarser to finer sorts, but the great urban

TABLE 3B

NRW : Changes in size and number of agricultural holdings 1965–71

1965				1971				Change in number of holdings 1949–71
Number	%	Total area (ha)	%	Number	%	Total area (ha)	%	
62 620	32·5	56 992	3·1	51 983	32·0	44 274	2·5	−51%
36 665	19·0	119 255	6·6	26 946	16·6	88 089	5·0	−57%
30 266	15·7	220 756	12·3	22 179	13·6	160 727	9·1	−51%
37 826	19·6	542 062	30·1	31 445	19·3	460 153	25·9	−11%
22 393	11·7	645 731	35·8	26 853	16·5	775 601	43·7	+41%
2 814	1·5	218 124	12·1	3 204	2·0	244 841	13·8	+21%
192 584	100	1 802 920	100	162 610	100	1 773 685	100	−40%

markets of Rhine-Ruhr continue to offer a lucrative outlet, a fact confirmed in Fig. 3.

But it is in livestock that some of the greatest changes have come about. The decline in horses from 219 000 in 1953 to 66 000 in 1971 reflects a trend for all size-classes of farm—by 1972 there were around 150 000 tractors in NRW. Beef cattle rose in total from 685 000 in 1953 to 1·1 million in 1971, a reflection of increased prosperity, but dairy cattle declined from 856 000 to 702 000 over the same period—one in which milk yields rose and the average herd size steadily increased. The main production areas continue to be in the Bergisches Land, conveniently located near the main market for fresh milk, and in the Lower Rhine and Aachen regions. Pigs increased in number from 2·3 million to 4·2 million over the same period and pork remains a major source of meat and meat products in NRW.

Agrarpolitik and agricultural restructuring

The circumstances so far outlined suggest unqualified gloom for the small or unspecialized farmer. Federal Germany adheres to a 'free market' or 'neo-liberal' economy and is therefore committed to the stimulation and ordering of market mechanisms and the stablizing of prices. Consequently, inefficient forms of economic activity have been forced out of production by competition, and existing problem regions have often seen their problems exacerbated. Much of the erosion of the labour force and the increased farm-size and specialization can be attributed to this competition, but the Federal and State governments have intervened to ease the individual peasant's problems and to co-ordinate such structural reform as land consolidation at community level.

Unlike many parts of Germany, NRW is not badly affected by land fragmentation, but a government department has to date undertaken a continuing programme of restructuring— affecting around 750 000 ha in NRW between 1948 and 1972—with the prime intention of creating machine-viable units. This *Flurbereinigung* has not only reduced the original number of separate plots by around two-thirds, but has also provided such improved rural facilities as new roads, drainage systems, and water supplies. Admirable as these programmes have been their cost has been considerable (1948–65 a total of 785 million DM) and the fear is that a second consolidation may become necessary because the original threshold size was set at 15 to 25 ha, whereas today's overall threshold is 30 ha.

In addition to the physical restructuring, the German Federal authorities have also offered financial inducement to those farmers who wish to retire early or to retrain and to those who wish to increase their holding size. Small to medium farmers in particular are attracted by such an inducement on condition that they enter into a long leasehold with another farmer, and the older man can accept an attractive retirement pension from the age of 55.

The Common Agricultural Policy

Finally one must consider, however summarily, the impact and implications of the E.E.C.'s Common Agricultural Policy. In part the C.A.P. solves some of NRW's problems, but it creates many new ones by legislation that forbids distortion of competition between members. E.E.C. farmers now receive guaranteed commodity prices—the cereal target price is, for example, based on Duisburg—and a system of farm import levies helps to finance a European Agricultural Fund charged with modernizing agriculture. At the root of the problem is the need to 'harmonize' supply (often in surplus) with demand, and to ensure prices artificially high enough to give the agricultural workforce an adequate standard of living. Such protection or market support has tended to delay the necessary modernization of European farming in general, and in 1968 an E.E.C. programme *Agriculture 1980* (popularly *The Mansholt Plan*) was published. This plan proposed a number of radical changes which are bound to affect much of NRW's farming and bring nearer the day when economic policy exercises a direct and rapid control, rather than an indirect and protracted effect, on the agrarian landscape. Minimum operational sizes for particular farming operations are specified, and loan funds are to be made available only to farmers and units capable of modernization; the movement away from dairying is to be encouraged by slaughter premiums; generous retirement bonuses and pensions are to be extended; overall some 5 million ha will be taken out of production to avoid costly surpluses which must presently be bought at 'intervention' prices by the authorities.

It would be unwise to predict the outcome of structural changes in NRW agriculture. It seems certain that intensification will continue, and that much marginal land will be converted to woodland or to recreational and other uses. At present rates of decline there would be no workers on the land in 25 years. This rate of transfer must diminish, even though the remaining 'free' peasants become in the process pawns of the bureaucrats. Perhaps the crucial development has been the peasant reaction to low returns: part-time farmer-commuters have increased in numbers and the spread of 'social fallowing' indicates how closely related is this phenomenon to upland areas with small farm-size (particularly the Siegerland, parts of the Sauerland, and the Eifel). (The term '*Sozialbrache*' [social fallow] or *Bauerwartungsland* has been coined to describe the phenomenon of agricultural land deliberately taken out of production for such reasons as insufficient free time, in cases where the farmer has paid work outside agriculture or where the land is economically marginal.) Concern over the ecological and social consequences of this economic decline has led the State Government urgently to reconsider the basic functions of rural areas, and in particular their value in cost-benefit terms as recreational environments. A policy of redistributing part of the social product to these areas through subsidies, to make some farmers conservators of the 'typical' agrarian landscapes, is under examination. Over the past decade the peasant exodus has been compensated for by an increase in population and a more marked rise in small-scale industries in the rural areas. The peasantry may soon find industrialists introducing factories to even the remoter districts, thereby hastening the day when such distinctions as townsman or countryman are themselves obsolete.

The cities and towns

Adjustment to change is a perennial problem of cities, for the three components of the mature townscape—town plan, building types, and land-use—are more often than not incongruous. Functional changes reflected in the competing and fluctuating urban land-use patterns seldom harmonize with the more rigid and conservative framework of street alignments and buildings. So much has been written about the German City that to attempt more than an outline of urban problems here would be unwise, but NRW provides many illustrations of how difficult it is to reconcile the inherited patterns with contemporary urban life. Sometimes the view is taken that history and tradition have exercised too powerful an influence on cities in West Germany, particularly in terms of post-war reconstruction. The argument is that traditionalism has shaped a retrospective rather than forward-looking society disinclined to accept change, even where it has become necessary. One American, for example, has written that 'Since the inception of the Industrial Revolution, Germany's cities have certainly been modernizing and adapting to the needs of modern technology and industrialism, but they have remained remarkably conservative . . . . Every stage of modernization seems to have been adjusted to existing inherited ways of life'. Others would argue that German cities are more than mere economically functional areas—containers and magnets with a spatial field of association, the one like the next—they are deliberately created expressions of individuality, continuity, and human values.

The distribution of cities and towns is a convenient point at which to introduce the problems of obsolescence. In particular the relationship of cities to the mainly rural districts over the past century demonstrates the fundamental shift of population and residence in NRW which occurred during industrialization. Rapid population growth, particularly in the Ruhr, is evident from the mid-nineteenth century as industry migrated from the hills to the coalfield and labour was drawn into a hitherto predominantly agricultural region particularly from Thuringia, Saxony, and Nassau. Between 1818 and 1925 the Ruhr's growth rate was greater than any other part of the present Federal German Republic, the consequences of which included an almost meteoric rise of towns like Oberhausen, Essen, and Bochum and their associated industrial housing sprawl. The rapidity of growth can be gauged by the fact that the average *annual* population increase in the modern Ruhr Planning Area (other parts of NRW in brackets) was 3 per cent between 1852–71 (0·8 per cent), 2·8 per cent between 1871–85 (1·3 per

TABLE 4
Population shift during industrialization

Population in	1871	1905	1939	1950	1961	1971
Cities	1 583 100	4 763 200	6 667 000	6 424 800	8 059 600	7 897 305
Landkreisen	2 673 400	3 716 200	5 268 000	6 772 600	7 841 900	9 240 447
Total	4 256 500	8 479 400	11 935 000	13 197 400	15 901 500	17 137 752

TABLE 5

TABLE 5

Urban growth in the Ruhr
(population in thousands)

Rank	1816	1852	1871	1905	1939	1971
1	Wesel (9·5)	Dortmund (13·5)	Essen (51·5)	Essen (231·4)	Essen (666·7)	Essen (691·8)
2	Duisburg (5·4)	Wesel (12·3)	Dortmund (44·4)	Duisburg (192·3)	Dortmund (542·3)	Dortmund (642·4)
3	Mülheim (5·0)	Mülheim (11·1)	Duisburg (30·5)	Dortmund (175·6)	Duisburg (434·6)	Duisburg (448·8)
4	Hamm (4·7)	Essen (10·5)	Bochum (21·2)	Gelsenkirchen (147·0)	Gelsenkirchen (317·6)	Gelsenkirchen (344·6)
5	Essen (4·5)	Duisburg (9·6)	Wesel (18·5)	Bochum (118·5)	Bochum (305·5)	Bochum (341·7)
6	Dortmund (4·3)	Borbeck (6·8)	Hamm (16·9)	Mülheim (93·6)	Oberhausen (191·8)	Oberhausen (244·9)

Source : Wiel, 1970.

cent), 3·4 per cent between 1885–95 (1·5 per cent), and 4·8 per cent between 1895–1905 (1·9 per cent). The transformation is even more impressive in noting the ranking and growth of the largest settlements in the Ruhr area before industrialization and at various stages up to the present (Table 5).

In comparatively few years, once important, though small, settlements like Wesel or Buer were eclipsed or absorbed into the new industrial towns. In order to set this transformation in context and to isolate those historic legacies which inconvenience the contemporary urban population, attention will be directed to the general implications of urban development up to 1939, and to the specific, unprecedented crisis which faced government and planners in 1945.

Historical factors

Urban settlements in NRW show a remarkable concentration along two broad axes, both of which can be traced back to pre-historic times. One, the Rhine, has enjoyed an importance as a routeway as much because of the roads—and much later the railways—which converge on or follow it as because of river transport. Several major cities like Bonn and Köln developed first under the Romans. The other axis, the *Hellweg*, lies along a spring-line just north of the Haarstrang and marks an ancient trade route which linked Duisburg and Köln, via Paderborn, with Magdeburg and Leipzig and more distant areas in the

TABLE 6

Urban growth outside the Ruhr
(population in thousands)

Town	1871	1905	1939	1950	1971
Köln	202·2	536·8	772·2	594·9	846·5
Düsseldorf	86·9	325·1	541·4	500·5	650·4
Wuppertal	179·1	378·0	401·7	363·2	416·7
Bonn	32·4	82·0	100·8	115·4	278·8
Krefeld	73·5	145·6	171·0	171·9	222·6
Münster	36·9	81·6	141·3	118·9	198·5
Solingen	56·0	120·8	140·5	147·8	176·9
Aachen	87·0	152·6	162·2	130·3	176·6
Bielefeld	32·2	93·2	130·0	154·3	167·1

Presseamt der Stadt Siegen

east. Many of these *Hellweg* towns—among them Duisburg, Essen, Bochum, Dortmund, Unna, and Soest—originated during the thirteenth century, typically as walled market settlements. This same linear pattern was repeated later in the south along the Ruhr Valley, when a string of small towns like Kettwig, Werden, Hattingen, and Schwerte grew up with the evolution of the coalfield from sporadic digging (earliest known date A.D. 1302) to organized mining from the mid-eighteenth century. In turn the staged extension of the Ruhr coalfield (Fig. 5) saw the traditional *Hellweg* axis towns converted to industrial growth points. The founding of successive roughly parallel settlement axes to the north followed; these are commonly differentiated as the southern and northern Emscher Zones (including Oberhausen, Essen, Gelsenkirchen, Wanne-Eikel, Castrop-Rauxel) and the Southern and Northern Lippe Zones (including Recklinghausen and settlements now absorbed into the municipalities farther south). These *Industriestädte* were oriented to specialist industry rather than to classic rural hinterlands and their transport linkages, whether road, rail or canal were west–east rather than north–south.

Elsewhere there existed several equally historic but isolated centres, of which Aachen, Münster, Siegen, and modern Wuppertal are good examples. Most of NRW's towns, whether isolated or catenary, have graduated through distinct evolutionary phases including the highly contrasted pre-industrial and industrial periods. In particular, the medieval period—an age marked by numerous town foundations and the emergence of 'free cities' and city leagues—has left a legacy of congested, unplanned city centres which clearly reflect the pressure on space, the complexity and small scale of occupational (particularly craft) divisions, and the restrictive influence of slow and primitive transportation which the Renaissance builders did little to change in form. Often the city walls prevented expansion, although some overcrowding was mitigated by overspill along the main roads or by the razing and rebuilding of fortifications.

Generally these trading cities were centred round a church and market-place, and the building fabric was replaced or added to in a piecemeal and unplanned way—although locally the planners of the Baroque era did seek (as in Krefeld) to impose new forms. The railway era had its main impact from the 1840s when communities were able to establish residential and industrial sub-centres. The growth of Köln illustrates the sequence: a small inner city (*Altstadt*) growing up around a Roman *castrum* and progressively walled-in until 1180; known in its day as 'the German Rome'; eclipsed in commercial power by the time of the Reformation despite being a Hansa Town, and unable for 700 years to demolish its inner fortifications until after the Franco-Prussian war of 1870. It subsequently built an outer ring of fortifications, allowing a small extension of the built-up area (*Neustadt*) between 1880–3; beyond lay a green belt cleared for artillery. With the development of railways and trams (and after about 1919 motor roads) growth and congestion accelerated—first in an inner suburban area (*Vorstädte*) beyond the fortifications and just across the river (up to 1888), and then before and after the First World War much more extensively as outer suburbs (*Vororte*) sprang up to the east and then the north of the city.

The Industrial Revolution brought with it the formidable expansion of town into country, much of the growth an unplanned and uncontrolled sprawl of pit colonies (*Zechenkolonien*), industrial plant and workers' dwellings, particularly in the Ruhr where it is best studied (Fig. 5, page 23). For over fifty years the Ruhr planning authorities have been trying to unscramble the

19

speculative and exploitive initiatives of its first 'developers' expressed in an inefficient mosaic of industry and housing.

The practical problems of the urban legacy manifest themselves at a variety of levels. The narrowness of streets, the transport bottlenecks, and the concentration of buildings near city centres are obvious; probably less obvious are the shortage of parks and recreational areas, the limited manoeuvrability of city administrations with weak tax bases founded on one-class/one-industry communities generally characterized by a low quota of tertiary employment, or the high cost of building sites or of rented accommodation. Yet perhaps more than any other factor, technological or social, it is the car which has made the traditional city out of date. Many Germans, however, argue that to demolish the bricks and mortar of a city is also to demolish a tradition. So demolition is often delayed.

Post-war reconstruction

Today's slum clearance and urban and transport replanning problems are as nothing compared to the scale of devastation which faced NRW in 1945. Something of the gravity of destruction is evident in Fig. 4, showing scarcely any major settlement escaping damage, although surprisingly only 131 477 civilians were killed in the NRW-area during the Second World War. Yet, argue some critics, out of this catastrophe could have come the planned reconstruction of NRW's urban and industrial fabric and a re-ordering of an already obsolete pattern of city regions and local government towards which Germany had been moving in the inter-war years. New towns (such as Marl-Hüls in 1936) had been founded, various planning regions and bodies had been set up by the Government, and German planners had, before 1945, begun planning for radical reconstruction.

Indeed, a new beginning had been envisaged by Roosevelt's and Churchill's advisers at Quebec in 1944, namely the 'pastoralizing' and 'de-industrializing' of Germany. Area bombing had cleared, in a sense for redevelopment, vast tracts of the old city centres; for industry, dismantling and reparations followed the surrender. The 'Morgenthau Plan' was never in fact implemented, for the Allied Powers soon realized that de-industrialization would have returned Germany to the economic straits which in 1932 had led to dictatorship. Given time, money, and the evacuation of half the population, such a transformation might have been achieved, but the need to rehouse people quickly meant that many plans were shelved as unworkable. With the wisdom of hindsight one can see that many mistakes were repeated or made afresh, and the chance of rebuilding the old cities in completely new idioms or even on green-field sites was lost. No money was available for grandiose replanning in a bankrupt state; Marshall Aid began only in 1948, the same year as the currency reform. Until 1949 no German *Land* existed as such, and legislation was inadequate to permit compulsory purchase and massive planning controls. Building materials were in short supply and the number of professional planners was quite inadequate for more than *ad hoc* solutions in most cities. Refugees and expellees made the crisis steadily more acute, as movement continued southward from the initial reception areas, particularly in Schleswig-Holstein. By the autumn of 1946 there were 700 000 refugees in NRW, mainly from the East and two years after the war the total had reached 1 million, most of whom were housed in emergency quarters. The final totals by province make impressive reading (Table 7), and today this element accounts for one in five of the total population.

In practical terms it was therefore easier to rebuild on the existing infrastructure of roads and

TABLE 7
Refugee and expellee population (by province)

Düsseldorf	1 061 893
Köln	414 348
Aachen	140 497
Münster	436 548
Detmold	384 995
Arnsberg	768 405
NRW total	3 206 686

of services like sewerage, water, and gas, much of which had survived bombing. So too the survival of cellars and basements, a normal feature of most existing housing, provided some shelter whilst families and communities practised self-help, salvaging material from the rubble. Many town administrations concentrated on the reconstruction of cultural features such as churches and theatres in order to raise public morale, and in reactivating public transport and other services. Comprehensive city-centre redevelopment was therefore the exception rather than the rule, although some municipalities like Düsseldorf and Bochum anticipated decisions which were eventually to be forced on most other NRW cities which had earlier merely rebuilt monuments to their past.

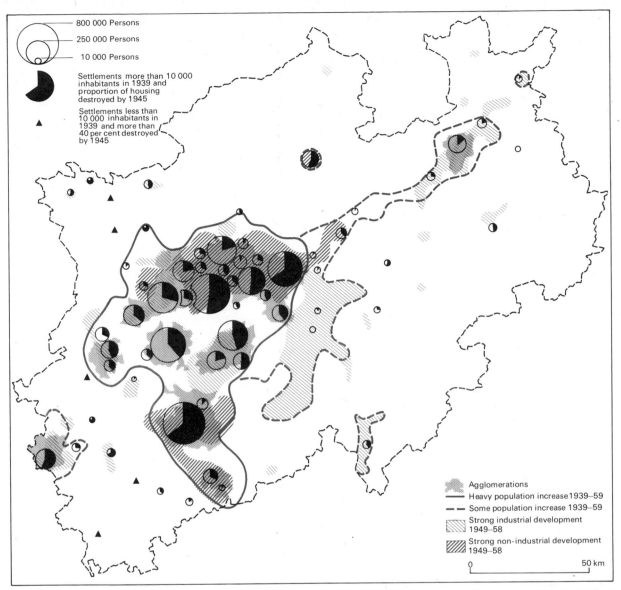

Fig. 4. War damage and post-war recovery

Legend:

- 800 000 Persons
- 250 000 Persons
- 10 000 Persons

Settlements more than 10 000 inhabitants in 1939 and proportion of housing destroyed by 1945

▲ Settlements less than 10 000 inhabitants in 1939 and more than 40 per cent destroyed by 1945

Agglomerations
— Heavy population increase 1939–59
--- Some population increase 1939–59
Strong industrial development 1949–58
Strong non-industrial development 1949–58

0   50 km

Source: Gassdorf and Langhans-Ratzeburg, 1952; Muller-Miny, 1959; Isbary *et al.* 1969

Today in many urban settlements of NRW the worst drawbacks of traditional forms have been ameliorated at great cost: ring roads and underground railways have been constructed, Central Business District (C.B.D.) redevelopment has been commonplace, suburban housing has been promoted. Relatively few sub-standard housing areas remain; in particular the slums of the typical *Altstadt* have largely disappeared, as have the many illegal and temporary houses erected after 1945. In the industrial towns particularly, effort is now concentrated on replacing the remaining tenements of the Wilhelminian era built between 1880 and 1918, and the industrial settlements built before 1880.

Fig. 4, which shows the main immediate post-war growth areas of population and industry still chiefly aligned as axial developments along the Rhine and Ruhr, helps to spotlight many of the problems and problem areas which will be considered in greater detail in the next chapter. The urban–rural dichotomy is striking.

21

3 Contemporary Problems

Many of the issues discussed in the following pages have arisen relatively recently, and in some cases with little warning. Obviously it would be impossible to mention here all, or even most, of NRW's contemporary problems, let alone the concatenation of effects attributable to any one of them. It could be argued that all NRW's regions are 'problem' regions of some sort; for example growth industries are just as likely to generate problems as static or declining industries. Some problems, like the structural reform forced on NRW's coal or steel industries, have reached crisis proportions. From being pillars on which the health of the economy depended these industries, particularly coal, became casualties of change. Other problems, like water supplies, transportation, conservation, and pollution are perennial, ubiquitous, similarly demanding of human and material resources, but more amenable to medium- and long-term solutions.

Coal in decline

Coal-mining in the Ruhr has traditionally been central in any discussion of German industry, whether pre- or post-war. Yet so far-reaching have been certain changes since 1957 that many standard texts require partial re-writing. Here the area mainly under discussion is the *Ruhrgebiet*, although the outlying Aachen and Ibbenbüren fields (Fig. 2) are involved.

At first sight, with reserves totalling at least 600 years' output at 150 million tonnes a year and talk of a world energy crisis, it might seem paradoxical that Germany should allow its main coalfield to run down when new markets are developing. By 1973 Belgium's coal-mining industry had contracted from 251 collieries at its zenith to a mere 19 units and in neighbouring Holland the last mine is scheduled for closure in 1975. In the Ruhr the largest total of collieries was 299 in 1857, exactly a century before the 1957 turning-point; the post-war peak of 148 collieries in 1954 had dwindled to 47 by 1972, with 4 more due to close in 1973. Economic and technological changes in combination have forced a substantial reduction in output and a rationalization of the industry, which in turn has led to massive pit closures and redundancies. At governmental level the politicians have therefore had to reconsider the role of domestic coal in the national energy policy, and the extent to which they can rehabilitate an ailing industry by subventions from public funds; at local level the Ruhr towns, faced by progressive depopulation and the erosion of their prosperity, have taken drastic steps to attract new industry, to redevelop mine property, and to diversify employment structure—in short to erase most of the evidence of the coal era and to create a new image for the Ruhr. Much of this problem is summed up by Table 8, which traces the relative shift in primary energy sources in the Federal Republic between 1958 and 1973.

Clearly there has been, despite a near-doubling of energy demand between 1957 and 1973, a serious fall in coal's relative share of the market as petroleum, and later gas, have made deep inroads into it. Since the Ruhr alone supplied 123—and the Aachen field another 7·6—of the 149 million tonnes of bituminous coal mined in 1957, the problems assumed crisis proportions almost overnight. To understand the element of surprise behind what became known as the '*Strukturkrise*', it would be useful to outline the general background up to the fateful year, 1957.

The Ruhr Coalfield falls into a series of five main basins (Fig. 5), generally deepening from south to north and characterized by an assemblage of grades ranging from anthracitic, through coking, to gas and domestic coal. In 1837 the first pit was sunk into the concealed coalfield at Essen, and only in 1840 did the Ruhr production first exceed 1 million tonnes. Water pumping, steam power generally and in particular the innovation of winding gear in 1852, brought about the relatively late start to mass production. Shafts had been sunk to an average depth of 40 m in 1800 and to 400 m in 1892; by 1973 they were deeper than 1000 m. On the surface, settlement and industry tended to locate in a definite chronological sequence, the supply of coking coal being decisive in the distribution of iron smelting and steel production. A particular feature, and eventually a vulnerable one, was the early development of industrial empires which integrated coal-mines, coke works, coal-based chemicals, and iron and steel production plant. Many towns were deformed economically and socially by this development, a tendency later

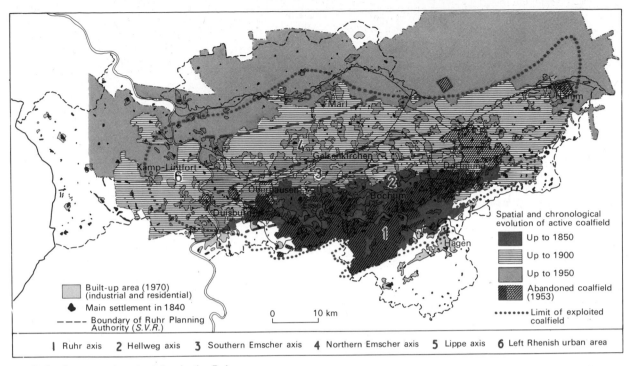

Fig. 5. Settlement and coal mining in the Ruhr

exacerbated by industrial 'cartelization'. In the case of Essen, for example, at its 'mono-economic' zenith in 1939, there were 40 000 miners and 13 000 steelworkers (42 per cent of the industrial workforce); Bochum had 32 000 and 22 000 respectively (44 per cent of the total).

The Aachen Coalfield, geologically a part of the 700 km² Aachen-Limburg-Kempen coalfield falls into two main basins mainly exploited near Alsdorf. Mining dates from the twelfth century, the modern industrial phase, however, from 1838. Although the number of collieries has fallen from 14 to 5, the area has always remained in the shadow of Aachen itself; often called the 'Grüne Revier' because of its pastoral setting, it has few of the Ruhr's social or economic problems. Ibbenbüren, with its one highly modern colliery, is located on the north-west edge of the Teuto-

burger Forest above a Carboniferous outlier of the Ruhr only 15 by 6 km in extent. It is now part of the Preussag concern and produces around 2·3 million tonnes annually.

Ruhr coal output reached its nadir in 1945, when production sank to 33 million tonnes, but the peace brought not only the need for rapid reconstruction but also the shortfall due to the loss of production areas chiefly to the east. (The Saarland was returned to Germany in 1967.) Under the military occupation, links between the coal and steel industries were sundered and the mines were geared up to meet expanding demand —until 1951 for general reconstruction, and from 1952 for the European Coal and Steel Community. As late as 1956 there were expectations of an energy shortage and the Ruhr stock-piled coal; production rose steadily until the 1957 total

TABLE 8
German energy sources 1958–73
(percentage of year's consumption)

	1958	1969	1971	1973 (estimate)
Hard coal	65	31	27	24
Brown coal	16	10	9	9
Oil	14	52	55	56
Natural gas	0·3	4	7	8
Hydro-electric power	3	3	2	2
Atomic energy	—	—	—	1

TABLE 9
Ruhr and Aachen coalfields: employment and production 1957–72

	Employment (thousands)			Production (million tonnes)		
	Ruhr	Aachen	F.G.R.	Ruhr	Aachen	F.G.R.
1957	494	34·5	604	123·2	7·6	149·4
1961	388	30·3	477	116·1	8·4	142·7
1966	287	24·1	354	102·0	7·4	126·0
1971	195	18·2	248	90·7	7·4	110·8
1972	175	15·6	220·6	83·3	6·3	102·5

Sources: (for 1957–71) *Statistik der Kohlenwirtschaft e.V.*, 1972 (for 1972) *Glückauf*, 1973.

reached 123·2 million tonnes, with 397 425 workers employed. But around 1957–8 the coal recession began, to be followed by steel recessions in 1958 and again in 1961.

What brought about such a change in coal's fortunes? Many of the causes can be linked with the world energy market and the German energy policy—or lack of it—until 1967. Productivity in the German coal-mines was generally not high enough to compete with low-cost producers such as the U.S.A. and Poland, and traditional Ruhr customers turned elsewhere. In the years after the Suez oil crisis shipping freight rates eased, American legislation led to an oil surplus and at about that time new producer countries began seeking outlets for greatly increased petroleum deliveries. Until the early 'fifties Germany had neither the foreign exchange nor the technical capacity to convert to oil. Indeed, production bottlenecks were retarding economic growth. From 1958 competition led to a major fall in oil prices, and many industries switched fuels. Throughout the period the coal producers were on the one hand facing rising costs in their mining operations and on the other the diminution of traditional markets either because of substitution or improved technology (as in the iron and steel industry or electricity generation) or even threatened evacuation of some plant to coastal sites. The associated human problems are summed up in Table 9, showing output and employment for the period 1957–72.

Such decline of the coal industry, no less than associated counter-measures, has had far-reaching effects on specific areas and communities and more generally on NRW as a whole. For the mining industry the crisis has brought radical restructuring. Total closure of German coal-mining was unthinkable, given the risks implicit in foreign control over the supply and price of more than half the Republic's energy requirements. To bring supply into line with demand, massive shrinkage was, however, unavoidable.

In the early years a sequence of uncoordinated pit closures, the continuing threat of bankruptcy, and massive government subsidies forced many painful changes. Shrinkage of the industry was most marked between 1962 and 1969, and the number of collieries in the Ruhr and Aachen coalfields fell to around 50. In 1968 the Federal Government had put forward its *Rheinstahl Plan*, aimed at concentrating the industry and injecting massive capital in an attempt to obviate continuous subsidy. Eventually in 1969 the formation of a holding company—the *Ruhrkohle AG (RAG)*—began to point the way from the abyss: twenty-four industrial concerns, including all the major steel producers, were included among its shareholders and all were vitally interested in the Ruhr's survival.

The reduction of output for the period 1956–70 was less (26·5 per cent) in Germany than in France (32·2 per cent), Britain (35·9 per cent), Belgium (61·6 per cent), or the Netherlands (63·4 per cent), but it was nonetheless formidable. Some 290 000 workplaces were lost in the Ruhr and Aachen coalfields over that period, many miners being displaced by early retirement or compensation; considerable numbers left the Ruhr permanently.

Concentration on fewer collieries, the operation of the Ruhr as a single unit, and the marked swing to mechanization—have yielded much improved productivity. Scarcely any mines now yield less than 1 million tonnes annually, and the rate per man-shift rose from 1·6 to 3·9 tonnes between 1957 and 1971. Where in 1956 only 12 per cent of coal-winning had been mechanized, the 1972 figure had risen to over 93 per cent, and the impending introduction of hydro-mechanical techniques (water-jet mining)—particularly well suited to thin and distorted seams—may mark a further crucial stage in the industry's fight for economic survival. Even if *RAG* succeeds in scaling its operations down still further to 40 or fewer collieries, with a combined output of 80

Some of the background detail of the classic pattern of iron and steel in NRW is important in any discussion of the processes which have reshaped the industry since the 1960s.

NRW has for long mined its own ore, particularly in the Siegerland and Eifel, and the early iron working tended to be dispersed in the uplands where water-power and charcoal were available. The development sequence is a familiar one, linked with crucial technical advances. In 1846 the first railway had reached the Ruhr at Duisburg from Köln and by 1847 it had been continued to Dortmund. Although coking coal, like iron ore, had been discovered in the Ruhr in the 1830s, it was not until 1849 that the first coke was made there. Between 1850 and 1870 the output of raw iron from the Rhenish-Westphalian area rose from 11 500 to 361 000 tonnes: the era of mass-production ensued; amongst the major techno-logical innovations were the Bessemer process (1862), the Siemens–Martin process (1869) and the Gilchrist–Thomas process (1879), and with their adoption came a steady expansion of production and product range.

Initially the distribution of blast furnaces was concentrated along the Ruhr Valley, and at the western (Duisburg, Oberhausen) and eastern (Dortmund) ends of the Ruhr. Although the period 1873–93 was one of industrial depression, it was one in which the minette ores of Lorraine and Luxembourg were first made into basic Bessemer steel (*Thomasstahl*). Industrial empires, such as those of Krupp and Thyssen, began to emerge with the integration of all aspects of iron and steel production, including tied mines. The period 1894–1914 saw a further expansion, with particular emphasis on 'heat economy' whereby heat and fuel costs were reduced by making smelting, converting, and rolling an uninterrupted process. During this period the main investment was along the Rhine at Duisburg and Rheinhausen and around Dortmund. There were important centres at Gelsenkirchen (1872) and Hagen (modernized around 1896), and there was also the isolated iron and steel industry of the Sieger-land around Hüttental where actual iron-ore mining ended only in 1964. The inter-war period was marked not only by depression, but also by loss of German territory, and expansion was restricted—although the Rhine–Herne Canal, opened in 1914, did offset the locational draw-backs of the central Ruhr.

The general pattern which emerged was one of pig-iron production mainly at either end of the Ruhr; this shift is shown in Table 10. The works, where these were not part of an integrated works, showed a wider distribution, and foundries, rolling mills, and pipe-making plant had an even more dispersed pattern. By 1945, of course, much of the iron and steel industry had been razed to the ground or was subsequently dismantled for reparations, and modernization was inevitably a feature of re-habilitation.

Since the post-war recovery, the NRW iron and steel industry, which accounts for about two-thirds of German steel output, has operated in a very difficult international market. Labour and coke costs have risen inexorably, the DM has been revalued three times since 1969, in 25 years the number of steel-producing countries has doubled to about 80, and the world trend towards very large integrated plant has been coupled with an intensely competitive world market. (By 1972, although Germany was still a major exporter selling around 25 per cent of its steel output abroad, 32 per cent of its domestic demand was met by imports; between 1960 and 1971 its share of world steel production fell from 10·3 to 7·2 per cent and of E.E.C. production from 46·7 to 39 per cent.)

Fluctuations in output since 1960 (Table 11) confirm the underlying problems facing a capital-intensive industry, hampered by an obligation to buy coke from *Ruhrkohle* at prices DM 10 per tonne above world prices in 1972, and currently operating at around 60 per cent of its capacity. Profitability and competitiveness have posed the major problems, and elimination of outmoded plant and surplus labour has had wide reper-cussions in a sector traditionally second only to coal in its employment of industrial workers. Because, like coal, the German steel industry has, with one exception, remained unnationalized, the different operation of firms like Thyssen, Hoesch, and Krupp makes any overview difficult. Undeterred by either pessimists or competitors, the steel-makers of NRW have adopted a variety of strategies to overcome their locational and cost disadvantages.

Organizationally the period since the early 1960s has been one of concentration. Mergers affected many great names after Thyssen linked

TABLE 10

Pig-iron production in the Ruhr
(% of total production for each area)

	1938	1950	1965
Western	48	42	55
Central	25	25	19
Eastern	27	33	26

Water-jet mining in the Ruhr. Contraction of the coal industry has been paralleled by increased mecha and experimentation at the face

million tonnes in 1975 and even 70 million in 1980, it still faces uncertainty, the more so in the light of political decisions which will be forced on the Government by the Arab oil embargo in 1973. In 1972 every tonne sustained a loss of DM 5·60, and 1977 could see cheaper British coal imports entering Germany duty-free. Yet given the remarkable success with which the people of the Ruhr District have divested themselves of a tradition without remorse or rancour, 1957–8 may ultimately be seen as an historical turning-point.

Iron and steel

Superficially the iron and steel industry of NRW might seem to be facing problems very similar to those which have brought about the retrenchment of coal-mining. Its main centres were chiefly dispersed throughout the Ruhr coalfield, and like coal the industry had tended to dominate the

life and character of whole citi it has faced the cold blasts competition, seen plant closu financial losses, and pessir questioning the long-term vi steel-making away from the c and economic changes have, coal, brought about a transfo a reduction of the industry. not being phased out in co stitutes; on the contrary, which increased by an av between 1955 and 1970, is 4·5 per cent per annum Germany as elsewhere stee a growth industry. Where since 1957, the graph of ir in NRW has, notwithst recessions, risen steadily tons in 1951 to around 5

TABLE 11

Output of iron and steel in NRW
(in million tonnes and as % of F.G.R. total)

	Pig-iron		Raw steel	
	million tonnes	%	million tonnes	%
1936	11·1	75	13·2	77
1960	18·0	70	24·7	72
1965	18·5	69	26·3	71
1970	22·2	66	30·5	68
1971	19·9	66	27·5	68

with Phoenix in 1964 and Hoesch with Dortmund-Hörde in 1966. Several distinct trends may be discerned: Thyssen's link with H.O.A.G. of Oberhausen made possible the unification of hitherto separate but virtually contiguous complexes; the transfer of interests between Thyssen and Mannesmann of Düsseldorf made the latter pre-eminent in steel pipe-making and underlined the advantage of product specialization; numerous small but specialist firms were absorbed and there was a general diversification into finished and semi-finished steel goods; finally, the logic of international integration was exemplified by the 1966 link between Hoesch and Hoogovens of Holland, subsequently transformed as a joint holding company (Estel N.V.) in 1972 with ambitious plans for a deep-water plant on the Dutch coast. What may prove to be the last major amalgamation in the current phase occurred in 1973 when Thyssen made a take-over bid for Rheinstahl of Essen, the combined production of which (over 13 million tonnes annually) would be second only to the British Steel Corporation in Europe. Given the creation in 1966 of selling agencies and their replacement in 1971 by four 'rationalization' groups, criticism of take-overs has not been muted and there is concern about free competition and monopoly control, no less than the concern felt about the political and social implications of the re-establishment of such massive industrial empires.

Technologically NRW has shared in international advances. The pre-war coke to pig-iron ratio of 1:1 had by 1973 declined to 1:2, with the likelihood of a further drop to 1:3—a disastrous development for *Ruhrkohle*. Daily output from the most modern, electronically-controlled type of blast furnace has quadrupled over the past decade. Although first introduced at Witten only in 1957, the L.D. 'oxygen' process now accounts for three quarters of all steel produced, and closures have affected basic converters and open hearth plant. Automation

and mechanization, particularly in the rolling mills, continues to reduce the labour force, put at 230 482 in 1971, although the 1966 figure of 239 585 demonstrates that concentration has had effects very different from those forced on coal mining. However, the drive towards economies of scale has made sharper the contrast between massive integrated steel plant, such as the *Thyssenhütte* at Duisburg-Hamborn, and the highly specialized 'mini'-steelworks outside NRW (of which there were 5 in 1972), operating at a capacity of up to 500 000 tonnes and based chiefly on electric-arc furnaces using scrap or direct reduction methods.

Given the land-locked situation of the Ruhr and the importance of giant ore-carriers today, it might seem an anachronism to persist in local iron making. Surprisingly, however, the transport-cost differential between Rotterdam and the Rhine-side works was only DM 2·50 per tonne of ore in 1972, and the importance of the local market for steel outweighed this disadvantage—Hoesch of Dortmund, for example, sells 80 per cent of its 7 million tonne output within a radius of 30 to 60 miles. Currently NRW's steelmakers are exploring possibilities of investing overseas in primary iron and steel production on or near the ore-fields, but more stringent anti-pollution laws are diminishing the attraction of coastal sites in Europe, and pipe-lines for solid raw-material transport may restore the balance in favour of market-oriented locations later this century.

Internally the NRW geography of iron and steel now reflects the way in which many immediate problems have been solved; a dichotomy exists between mass-production at a few sites, chiefly along the Rhine (*Westruhrhüttenwerke*, plus the smaller *Ostruhrhüttenwerke* around Dortmund) and the smaller-scale manufacture of high-quality steels and steel products at more dispersed locations like Krefeld, Remscheid, and Bochum. The short-term problem remains the

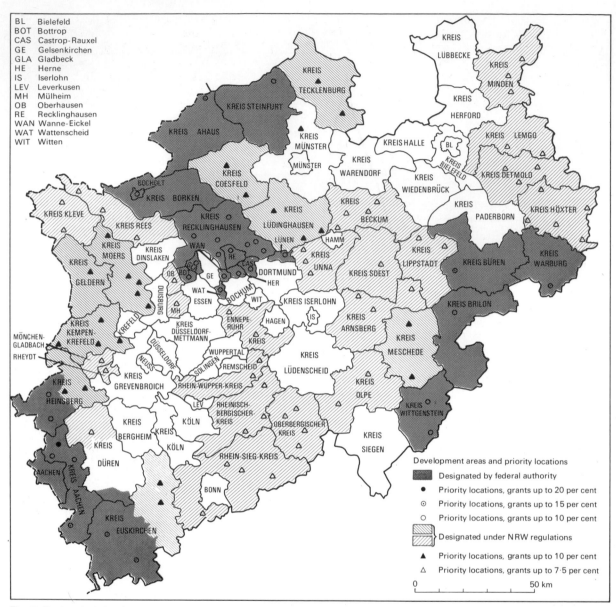

Development areas and priority locations

Designated by federal authority

● Priority locations, grants up to 20 per cent

⊙ Priority locations, grants up to 15 per cent

○ Priority locations, grants up to 10 per cent

Designated under NRW regulations

▲ Priority locations, grants up to 10 per cent

△ Priority locations, grants up to 7.5 per cent

0   50 km

Fig. 6. Designated development grant areas

Source: Gesellschaft für Wirtschaftsförderung

fixed price of Ruhr coke, and in the medium-term the problem is of a future which has, due to low profits since 1970, been built on shallow investment foundations. Cost inflation is now largely a matter amenable only to deliberate intervention by the Federal Government.

New industries for old

Since the mid-1950s the employment situation in NRW has clearly undergone radical change. Much of this was involuntary and the outcome of internal decline or stagnation in traditional industries or of the external challenge from other industrialized *Länder*. Pit closures resulted in the most obvious redundancy of both labour and industrial land, but other sectors, such as textiles (which shed over 60 000 workers between 1960 and 1969), contributed to a massive unemployment threat.

In-migration exceeded out-migration only until 1961–2, since when NRW's slow increase in population has been made possible only by natural increase and the in-migration of foreign workers. In 1966 the number of out-migrants 'peaked' at 230 000; in and between 1968 and 1970 there was a compensatory inflow of 206 000 *Gastarbeiter* to bring their total in employment to 517 376; by 1970 between 5 and 10 per cent of the workforce in towns like Remscheid, Köln, Krefeld, Düsseldorf, Hagen, and Duisburg was non-German, the main countries of origin being Italy, Yugoslavia, Turkey, Greece, and Spain. Much of the population exodus was from the decaying agglomeration cores, and the new-found mobility of labour threatened to deplete NRW of some of its most highly skilled, and generally younger, workers. Accordingly urgent programmes were formulated by both government and local authorities to create a better working and living environment, chiefly by infrastructural investment, by providing vocational re-training facilities, and by attracting new industries for old.

Investment in infrastructure and the overall principles and objectives of planning will be discussed elsewhere, but it is important to note that the State and *Land* provide financial assistance under the aegis of the *Rahmenplan* (Framework Plan) and pass associated legislation. The Federal Government has designated certain Development Areas in which grants can be made, particularly for the setting up, re-location or expansion of manufacturing establishments or the promotion of tourism. Development Areas and priority locations are illustrated in Fig. 6, which distinguishes Federal- and State-assisted localities, and the maximum investment grants available. NRW also grants low interest loans, but the overriding consideration has been to achieve 'balanced' economic growth, and assistance has normally been extended only where investment exceeded DM 500 000 per enterprise.

The *Land* government has actively promoted change through the semi-official *Gesellschaft für Wirtschaftsförderung*, an industrial and investment advisory service, set up in 1960, and particularly active since 1965. Around 1960, Ford Motors (already making vehicles in Köln) and Kaiser Aluminium had sought to locate in NRW, but site and other problems had diverted their investment to Genk (Belgium) and Koblenz respectively. Since 1960 the *G.f.W.* has advised more than 3100 firms, and between 1965–70 over 300 new firms located in the *Land*, dominated by the chemical and mineral-oil processing, non-ferrous metal, electro-technical, and vehicle-building industries, as shown in Table 12.

The extent of land available for industrial redevelopment is most obvious in the former coal-mining areas: the case of Gelsenkirchen well illustrates the great extent of the mine workings at their peak, as does the whole map of the Ruhr (Fig. 5). Individual local authorities were able to negotiate transfers between mine owners and intending industrial developers on a scale which would have been unthinkable before the energy crisis. Of about 31 130 ha of land scheduled for industrial use, only 60 per cent was taken up at the start of 1970, and an inventory compiled with redevelopment in view by the Ruhr Planning Authority (*S.V.R.*) is highly informative (Table 13).

Ownership of land by the mining companies is a dominant feature, and in the core area of the Ruhr this form of ownership rises to about 42 per cent. Theoretically the coal owners were therefore in a position to veto industrial development, but in practice subsidence presented problems to investors who might have been forthcoming. (*Industrial* land prices are relatively low in NRW by German standards—about DM

TABLE 12

Enterprises locating in NRW 1965–70

Industrial Class	Firms advised	Firms locating	Weighted % of new employment
Chemicals and mineral-oil processing	141	27	17·3
Non-ferrous metal	31	9	9·8
Electro-technical	131	30	9·5
Vehicle-building	45	13	7·9
Mechanical engineering	234	33	7·4
Plastics	124	25	6·2
Metal fabrication	92	27	5·6
Other (mainly tertiary)	225	35	5·4
Paper manufacture	61	14	5·2

Source : Gesellschaft für Wirtschaftsförderung, 1970

Owner		Area (ha)	% of total
Coal mines		3 496	28
Iron and metal industry		1 663	13
Chemical industry		613	5
Public:			
Local Authority	1 826		
Land	189		
Federal Government	304	2 319	19
Agriculture	——	2 919	23
Other		1 512	12
Total		12 522	100

Source: *Industriestandort Ruhr*, 1970.

35 per m² in Essen, and DM 4 in rural areas in 1972.)

Taking Germany as a whole there are fairly clear-cut categories of high-growth and declining industries. NRW had a large share of those in the declining group: food, drink and tobacco, glass, mining, textiles, saw milling, and timber manufacture. Others, including iron- and steel-making, steel manufactures, metal goods, and clothing are expected to grow at or below average rates. Most highly sought after are those high-growth industries which tend to promote spatial associations with other groups. These include the plastics, electro-technical, chemical, mechanical engineering, and mineral-oil refining industries. To identify key industries is one matter, but to attract new plant is quite another, and local authorities have enjoyed varying success (Table 12).

That a shift in employment by sector has occurred is very clear from the focus of greatest change—the Ruhr Planning Area—over the period 1950–70. Ignoring the small primary sector, there was a decrease from 63·4 to 58·4 per cent in the total labour employed in the secondary sector, mainly balanced by a rise from 32·1 to 40·1 per cent in the tertiary. NRW's employment situation in 1970 is summarized by sector in Table 14 and the industrial groups are shown in detail in Fig. 7.

Behind the relatively slight sectoral shifts for NRW is a history of considerable achievements at local level in 'modernizing' the secondary sector. Yet rarely has unemployment exceeded 3 per cent, and by 1973 most towns were back to 1 per cent or less. Bochum, which in 1952 had had 55 per cent of its industrial workers in coal-mining and another 25 per cent in steel, is a case in point. It had been a major recipient

of investment in mine rationalization, yet in 1960 there began a ruthless programme of pit closures, putting over 50 000 men out of work between 1958 and 1968. A major television manufacturer moved to Bochum in 1956, and negotiations begun in 1960 led to the first Opel car being produced there in late 1962; today over 16 000 workers are employed in two main car factories. Work on the new Ruhr University started in 1964, which with almost 20 000 students gave a great boost to the tertiary sector. Elsewhere in the Ruhr there have been other major successes. Gelsenkirchen, further north and a centre of heavy industry and chemicals, faced a similar decline; then after 1945 much of the former clothing industry of Breslau (Silesia) settled in the city, and by 1969 over 40 clothing firms had

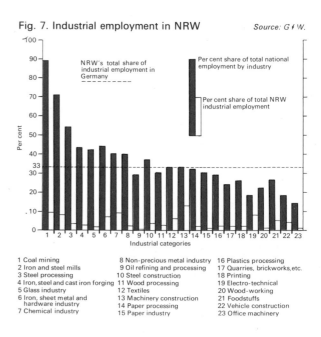

Fig. 7. Industrial employment in NRW   Source: G & W.

1 Coal mining
2 Iron and steel mills
3 Steel processing
4 Iron, steel and cast iron forging
5 Glass industry
6 Iron, sheet metal and hardware industry
7 Chemical industry
8 Non-precious metal industry
9 Oil refining and processing
10 Steel construction
11 Wood processing
12 Textiles
13 Machinery construction
14 Paper processing
15 Paper industry
16 Plastics processing
17 Quarries, brickworks, etc.
18 Printing
19 Electro-technical
20 Wood-working
21 Foodstuffs
22 Vehicle construction
23 Office machinery

Sector	NRW total	NRW %	Ruhr %
Primary	297 000	4·3	1·2
Secondary	3 876 400	55·7	58·4
Tertiary	2 789 200	40·0	40·4
Total	6 962 600		

TABLE 14
NRW employment 1970

moved there, including the Eurovia Textile concern in 1966. Further, the important chemical industry, begun in 1872 diversified into petro-chemicals after 1945, and the establishment of Olefin plant (1967) was particularly significant.

Such lists could be extended to include plant such as the aluminium smelter at Voerde near Dinslaken, the giant American-owned synthetic fibre factory at Unna, the expansion of petro-chemical industry along the Rhine near Wesseling, or numerous innovations throughout NRW as a whole. The coal crisis of the Ruhr, followed by the more general recession of 1966–8 forced changes upon the workforce and intervention by the government. In the intervening period the most marked development in terms of industrial employment has been the above-average growth on the fringes of the agglomerations. Increased commuting numbers and distances have also tended to upset the tradition of a century, whereby workplace and residence were effectively identical. But, above all, there appears to be a growing awareness amongst industrialists and planners of the importance of spatial and functional linkages between industries, and the fine balancing of inputs and outputs. The locational effect of these linkages is likely to be of growing importance in the more mobile, high-growth groups exemplified by the science-based or engineering and metal-using industries.

Transport

Given the change and growth which has affected NRW since 1951 in particular, it would be surprising had the existing transport network not come under increasing strain. Where the network has become inefficient in terms of time or cost, the remedies have generally excluded radical restructuring in favour of modification, adaptation or extension. The catalogue of causes and effects surrounding the 'transport problem' is one familiar to most densely-settled industrial countries: motor vehicles in particular have brought existing road networks to the limit of their capacity and captured passenger and goods

Gelsenkirchen-Buer: Veba Chemical Company's petroleum refinery and the 1380MW coal-fired Scholven power station

Presseamt der Stadt Gelsenkirchen

	Outgoing (million tonnes/percentage)				
Year	Rail	Waterway	Road (non-local)	Pipeline	Total
1950	137·4/n.a.	35·8/n.a.	n.a.	none	—
1955	172·9/70·5	49·9/20·3	22·6/9·2	none	245·4/100
1960	179·2/64·9	68·9/25·0	28·0/10·1	none	276·1/100
1965	139·2/58·6	62·7/28·3	35·5/15·0	none	237·4/100
1970	166·1/59·8	69·9/25·2	41·8/15·0	none	277·8/100
1971	151·4/57·7	68·6/26·1	42·5/16·2	none	262·5/100
	Incoming (million tonnes/percentage)				
1950	104·1/n.a.	19·9/n.a.	n.a.	none	—
1955	135·7/67·4	44·3/22·0	21·2/10·5	none	201·2/100
1960	137·3/58·8	59·2/25·4	24·9/10·7	12·0/5·1	233·4/100
1965	102·9/46·1	62·6/28·0	32·6/14·6	25·3/11·3	223·4/100
1970	127·9/46·3	76·7/27·8	37·3/13·5	34·1/12·4	276·0/100
1971	117·6/44·8	71·9/27·4	38·6/14·7	34·3/13·1	262·4/100

Source: Die Verkehrsentwicklung, 1972.

traffic from other media. The private ownership of cars has increased population mobility and commuting levels, and the flexibility of road transport has transformed traditional flow patterns. But technological advances have also tended to run ahead of existing frameworks, and it has proved difficult to harmonize the interests of road, rail, and water traffic and to integrate regionally the transport plans of individual administrative areas. Any decline in public transport provision exacerbates alike the unattractiveness of life and work in the older built-up areas and in the most isolated rural communities.

Paradoxically the engineers and planners have never had such a wealth of demand data and theoretical models on which to assess the cost-benefit of alternative systems, yet ideal solutions are frustrated by reality. Whether the system is being programmed for commuter 'rush hours', raw material transport or international exchanges, bottlenecks and congestion are a constant reminder that transport provision is often incapable of meeting the demands placed on it. It is therefore important to distinguish between what is desirable and what is practicable, between long-term modernization in the *Land* as a whole, and remedial intervention in the form of heterogeneous local measures.

Problems on the national and European scale
To an exceptional degree NRW is affected by the Europeanization of markets and transportation. Connectivity and integration are implicit in developing relationships with the great metropolitan agglomerations, like Randstad-Holland or Rhine-Main, which are redefining the geography of Europe. A consequence of this internationalization of transport is the concentration of roads (*Europa-Strassen*), canals, and railways, which have made Rhine-Ruhr a nodal point. By 1971 NRW possessed 896 km of motorways and another 5710 km of Federal roads (excluding the 21 550 km of Class A and B roads), 6437 km of railway lines and 698 km of riverine or canalized waterways, together serving Germany's major exporting *Länder* and the through-traffic of its E.E.C. partners.

Table 15 provides a summary of goods movements over the period 1950–70, bringing out in particular the decline in the railways' share, the steady hold of water transport on about a quarter of all tonnage, and the recent but growing role of pipelines. These tendencies are even more clearly exemplified by international movements to and from NRW for the year 1970: nearly 33 per cent of goods tonnage were moved in sea-going vessels, 25 per cent by barge, 23 per cent by pipeline, 10 per cent by railway and only 9 per cent by road. The international character and importance of some of the NRW transport network is exemplified by the Rhine: in the early 1970s only one third of all Rhine traffic passing Emmerich was German.

Comparative study of the transport network before and after the division of Germany helps to explain the need for far-reaching alterations. The railways of NRW were mainly completed by 1865, and from 1924 state control integrated them as an element in national policy. Similarly the canals and rivers had been shaped as an integral part of the larger transport network of the *Reich*, the Dortmund-Ems Canal was completed by 1899, the Rhine-Herne Canal by 1914 and the Lippe Canal by 1930. The first German motorways were operative by 1935, being based on a six-highway grid with mainly north to south and west to east axes.

After 1945 the first problem was reconstruction: for example, 57 per cent of NRW's roads were damaged and 38 per cent of its bridges destroyed. Soon after began the 'motor explosion': from a 1948 figure of 0·3 million motor vehicles the total in 1971 had soared to 4·4 million. A major factor in containing this transport revolution has been the enlargement of the *Autobahn* network and the construction of urban motorways. In 1950 the NRW motorways totalled 328 km; by 1961 they rose to 470 km and in 1971 they extended over 896 km. This expansion has had far-reaching consequences for NRW, in particular the opening up of new growth axes. Where in 1939 the motorways had only linked Köln via the Ruhr with Hannover, today most of the major cities are directly connected to the European system. In recent years there have been significant advances into peripheral areas of low population: the *Hansalinie* (1968) now links the eastern Ruhr with Hamburg via Münster, the *Sauerlandlinie* (1972) cuts through the *Süderbergland* to join the eastern Ruhr with Frankfurt, and other axes like the *Hollandlinie* (Ruhr–Rotterdam) and the projected *Eifel Autobahn* (Köln–Trier–Luxembourg) seem likely to help towards the decentralization of both population and industry.

Current road problems at *Land* level can be summarized in terms of the five main objectives scheduled in the NRW Development Programme 1970–5, namely, the elimination of bottlenecks in the road network, the improvement of links between agglomerations and their hinterlands, the opening-up of underdeveloped areas, the integration of the network with the European system, and provision for recreational traffic. By about 1990 the planned road network will bring most areas within 10 km of motorways or similar roads, and current tasks include the building by 1975 of 830 km of dual-carriageway, 320 km of Federal roads and 2000 km of *Landstrassen*.

Inland waterways do not pose major problems as such, although the development of the 1000 to 1350 tonne Europa Barge and the massive *Schubboot*, capable of pushing six or more 3000 tonne units on the Rhine, requires considerable

Presseamt der Stadt Bochum

Urban motorway and one of the Opel car factories, Bochum

improvements, particularly the deepening of canals, which now have a normal minimum depth of 2·70 m.

German railways have faced the decline of basic industries like coal and the universal problem of running at a loss, although the NRW Government has consistently opposed a major closure programme. Nevertheless the railways have benefited from electrification programmes, the development of container terminals and the continuing elimination of level-crossings (some 50 in NRW). With two international airports at Düsseldorf and Köln-Bonn, and a third planned for the Münster area, the *Land* is well served, although the siting of regional airports poses greater difficulties.

Problems at the local level

Each community has its own peculiar set of problems, whether due to isolation or congestion, but the increased commuter movements, the growth of employment in the tertiary sector, and the continuing concentration of settlement all necessitate the formulation and implementation of a coherent public transport programme. Around 90 per cent of all journeys are still made by public transport, and the expectations are that demand will increase until at least 1990. To reduce pressure from private cars in the agglomerations a new concept of public transport has been evolved. A rapid transport system involving inter-urban railways (*S-Bahn*) has been inaugurated, and will ultimately extend from Siegburg in the south via Köln and Düsseldorf, through the Ruhr and along the Wuppertal/

33

Hagen axis, to outliers like Marl and Hamm. Linked with the *S-Bahn* will be an interconnecting network, in part underground, of *Stadtbahnen* (municipal railways) both in the Ruhr and between some cities on the Rhine; feeder services will be provided by motor buses. The network will in turn link up with the main inter-city routes of the Federal Railway (*Fernbahn*). This hierarchy will underpin the long-term aim of ordering settlement on the principles of central place theory, and complement the flexibility of individual, motorized movements along other roads.

Gelsenkirchen well illustrates many of the transport problems facing Ruhr cities. Unified in 1928, it grew from two old villages (Alt-G.K. and Buer) about 7 km apart, separated by the marshy Emscher Valley. In common with other settlements in the Ruhr the main transport links took on a west–east orientation, the first railway arriving in 1847; by 1970 there were 18 stations in the city of 350 000 people. Local roads radiated from the old cores to developing pit villages. The completion of the Rhine-Herne Canal and the building of a port to serve the industrial zone tended to perpetuate the bi-polarity of Gelsenkirchen, and four main through routes, including the Oberhausen motorway built in 1937 and the partially-completed *Emscherschnellweg*, have done nothing to remedy the poor north–south linkage. Wartime destruction permitted some restructuring, but in 1972 the road on which speedy access to recreational areas to the north and south depends, was still under consideration as part of a projected Ruhr–Ostfriesland motorway. However, in 1972 work began on the first stage of the *Stadtbahn*, largely underground, to link Wattenscheid with Erle. Eventually this urban railway will bring about 85 per cent of the population within 500 m of some station; the very high cost (up to ten times greater than equivalent motorway lengths) will be offset by the saving of land and avoidance of demolition.

Elsewhere local problems have generated a wide range of solutions and secondary effects. Notable among these is the case of Wuppertal, a linear city constricted by its valley setting: the suspension railway (*Schwebebahn*), built in 1900, carries daily 45 000 passengers in its 13 km length mainly above the winding Wupper. In 1970 Wuppertal overcame the problem of access from the city centre to the *Autobahn* network by building Europe's first two-storey tunnel (the *Kiesbergtunnel*). Other examples could include the fundamental changes brought about by new Rhine bridges as at Emmerich, Düsseldorf or Bonn, or the renaissance of hitherto isolated, relatively inaccessible towns like Siegen as a direct result of motorway construction. The shortening of transit times reflects the enormous, if costly, success of the roads programme and the irreversible changes it has generated. Modern

TABLE 16

Water Resources

Basin	Area (km²)	Precipitation (mm)	Population (December 1968)	% pop. with public water supply	% pop. with public sewerage	Reservoirs	Major sewerage works
Weser	4956	811	1 252 000	79	60	none	9
Ems	4125	755	1 236 000	71	81	none	6
Bocholter Aa and others	1835	754	336 000	62	75	none	4
Lippe	4865	828	1 518 000	90	72	1	8
Ruhr	4439	1039	2 471 000	91	83	25	9
Emscher	855	776	2 766 000	98	93	1	6
Wupper	824	1222	957 000	95	74	19	5
Itter	111	992	186 000	98	69	none	5
Niers	1331	716	594 000	95	77	none	2
Issel	351	724	58 000	61	57	none	none
Schwalm	250	733	87 000	98	71	none	3
Rheingraben-N	2030	707	2 121 000	97	87	none	6
Rheingraben-S	920	670	1 584 000	99	84	none	10
Sieg	2240	1000	667 000	97	48	7	7
Erft	1953	631	581 000	99	79	2	5
Rur	2153	822	920 000	99	75	9	6

Source: Entwicklungsprogramm Wasserwirtschaft, 1969.

road-building more than ever before now shapes land-use instead of being subordinated to it, and in no other problem area is the scale and rapidity of innovation more striking.

Water supply and water pollution

When the 'romantic' Rhine came to be labelled 'Europe's sewer' it needed little effort to persuade people in general that the environment was under intolerable pressure and conservation became a major political issue almost overnight in Germany. In many ways water epitomizes the dilemma of how far man ought to seek control of nature: water tends to be taken for granted until supply falls short of demand and it becomes a scarce resource, and similarly surface waters quickly indicate to the layman the aesthetic and ecological effects of pollution. This section will discuss some aspects of water supply and demand—and in particular the organization of water resources—and will then turn to pollution of waters and the more general issues of *Umweltschutz* (conservation). It will show to what a high degree the drainage network has become man-made and the water-flow regulated.

Fig. 8. Generalized hydrology, forest cover, and reservoirs

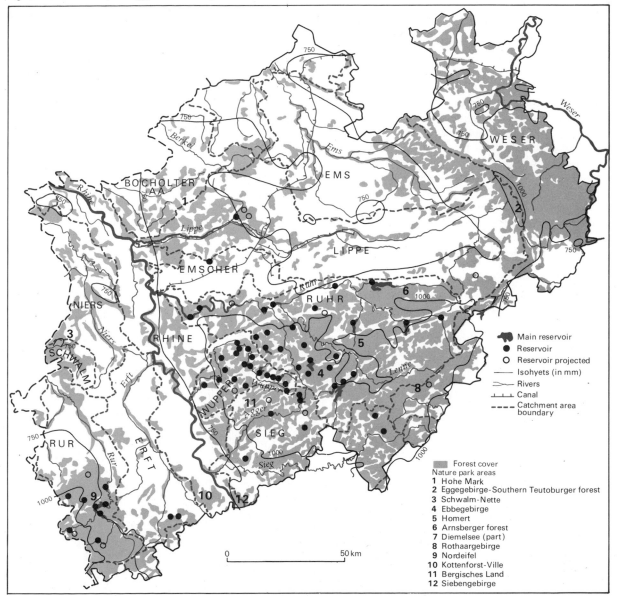

35

Water supply comes from two main sources: the run-off from the upland areas and the groundwater which tends to accumulate in the sands and gravels of valleys like the Rhine. Additional supplies come from mine-workings, opencast pits, and the purification and recycling of effluent. The water economy is perhaps best summarized in terms of the size and yield of the main river basins, and the use to which their waters are put by the construction of reservoirs, filtration plants, and sewage works. Table 16 should be read in association with Fig. 8, which illustrates the concentration of reservoirs in areas enjoying over 1000 mm of precipitation annually, chiefly in the well-wooded uplands of the Sauerland, Bergisches Land, and Eifel. Of an overall average precipitation of 836 mm in catchments totalling 32 238 km² yielding 28·4 billion m³ of water, 34 per cent is lost by transpiration, 20 per cent is lost by evaporation, 9 per cent enters groundwater reserves and 37 per cent becomes run-off.

Demand for water tends to rise by 0·5 to 1 per cent annually, and a major post-war problem has been to keep pace with the increased consumption by communities newly linked to public supply: in four of the six *Regierungsbezirke* existing until 1972 practically the whole population had piped water, whereas in Detmold and Münster—areas of highly dispersed settlement in parts—the figures fell to 80 and 86 per cent respectively. Demand from industry places very heavy strains on resources: the chemical industry absorbs about 26 per cent of the water consumed by the industrial sector, the equivalent of all domestic consumption, the iron and steel industry another 20 per cent and the coal mines 40 per cent, much of which is pumped from mine-workings. Because of such severe competition for limited resources and the close link between water supply and effluent, NRW has pioneered many aspects of the organization and technology of water supply and purification, and its hydrology is manipulated as a system in which extraction and replenishment within and between river basins is commonplace.

Internally NRW falls into sixteen main river basins, although for planning purposes the division is into eleven main regions: in turn about 1300 corporate water users are organized under the aegis of the water associations or co-operatives discussed below. By the turn of the century it was realized that the complexity of the water-cycle and the requisite harmonization of water supply, flood prevention, and sewage disposal demanded overall management. In 1897 the Ruhr Reservoirs Association (*R.T.V.*) was founded on a voluntary basis, and in 1904 the first of a series of acts led to the setting up of water associations with very similar constitutions and powers. These authorities are autonomous public corporations, empowered to assess the contributions levied on all water users in proportion to direct or indirect benefits received; municipal and industrial users are obliged to become members, but in turn participate directly in the organization, which has the power to plan, build, and operate installations.

To take one example, the Emscher Co-operative, founded in 1904, involved a relatively small but almost totally built-up area of 855 km², affected to such a degree by progressive mining subsidence that serious drainage and public health problems made comprehensive planning the only solution. Its achievements have made it a classic example of intervention. Because of subsidence, the mouth of the Emscher was shifted 2·8 km northwards between 1906–10, and today its confluence is 9 km north of the original confluence with the Rhine. To date, around 365 km of the Emscher and its tributaries have been widened, deepened, and regulated to ensure effective drainage, and in the process the river has been shortened by one third. Mining has created such impeded drainage that only a polder-landscape, complete with dykes and pumping stations, ensures the continued settlement of 32 per cent of the catchment. Seventy-seven pumping stations artificially drain at a capacity rate equivalent to 340 m³/s, or half the Rhine flow at Köln. Re-aligned and flowing along conduits, the Emscher functions as an open sewer in which the effluent of around 24 municipal and industrial plants drains westward after primary (mechanical) purification. Transfers from the Ruhr ensure sufficient dilution water in periods of low discharge. Construction of a massive plant at *Emschermündung* near Dinslaken, begun in 1966, will eventually undertake the secondary (biological) purification of the entire Emscher Region.

A second well-documented authority is the *R.T.V.*, legally constituted in 1913, and concerned with providing around 70 per cent of the *Ruhrgebiet's* water demand (the remainder coming from the Rhine and the Lippe). Because of the fluctuations in the Ruhr's discharge, an early objective was regulation of flow by reservoir construction: the Lister Dam (21·6 million m³) and Möhne Dam (134·5 million m³) were finished in 1912 and 1913 respectively, and since then storage capacity has been raised to about 492 million m³, notably by the completion of the

Bigge Dam (171·7 million m³) in 1965. This water is not generally pumped directly to users but is used to replenish the Ruhr, from which in turn about 100 waterworks extract. About 40 per cent of the annual abstraction of 1200 million m³ is pumped to the catchments of the Wupper, Emscher, and Lippe—about 17 per cent of their mean annual flow. Related to the *R.T.V.* is the *Ruhrverband* (Ruhr River Association), the specific task of which is to construct and operate the plants necessary to prevent pollution of the Ruhr;

the most striking of its achievements are the four impounding lakes (clarifying basins) strung along the lower Ruhr valley at Lakes Hengstey, Harkort, Baldeney, and Kettwig, together with about 110 water purification plants. Both in the upper catchments, and specifically in the Ruhr valley, reservoirs such as these play a vital role in recreation.

In overall terms the reservoir construction programme (Fig. 8), expected to reach a capacity of 1183 million m³ by 1986, demonstrates the

Fig. 9. River pollution 1965

Source: Wasserwirtschaft, 1969

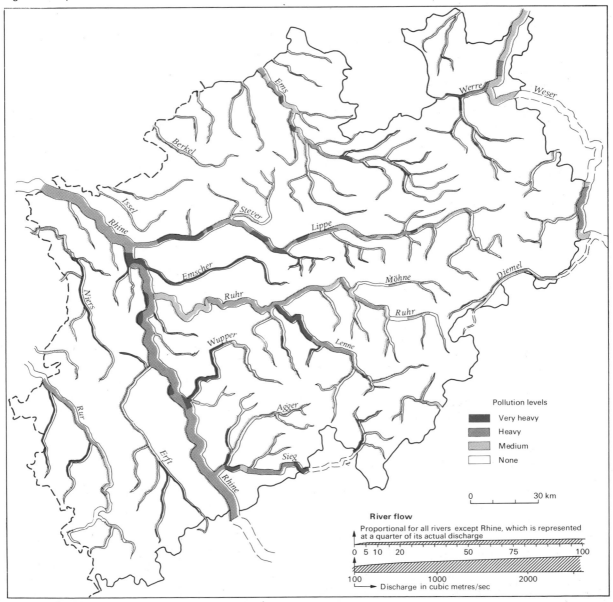

continuing problem of meeting demand and regulating floods: 1947 and 1959 were serious drought years, 1946, 1956, and 1965 conversely serious flood years. Between 1949 and 1968 fourteen dams were finished in NRW with a capacity of 410 million m³, but construction work continues not only to supply the Ruhr but also such areas as the southern Münsterland and Paderborn (*Aa* Reservoir), Aachen (*Wehebach*) and Siegen (*Obernau*). Planned investment in the *Wasserwirtschaft* announced for the period 1969–73 totalled 5542 million DM, but significantly over half was directed towards sewage works, which will arrest further deterioration of river water quality. Such water can be processed by filtration plants—the Ruhr is said to be re-used ten times in its length in a dry year—and is often cheaper than stored water in a situation now marked by virtual exhaustion of potential reservoir sites and a construction cost of 5–6 DM per m³ of reservoir capacity. Were it not for contamination, flooded mine-workings could constitute a new form of storage, as could also the open-cast workings of the Brown Coalfield.

Pollution as such is a major and long-standing problem in NRW (Fig. 9) and the subject demands a more extended treatment than is feasible here. Traditionally there was a belief in the 'self-cleansing' power of rivers, but the fouling of the Rhine, highlighted by the fish disasters of 1969 and 1971, convinced *laissez-faire* elements of the immediacy of this problem. The sheer magnitude and diversity of effluent from industrial, domestic, and agricultural sources demanded a progressive programme of control and rehabilitation. Not only are the Rhine waters in particular grossly loaded with toxic substances from heavy metals to DDT, but new pollutants also threaten: radioactive wastes are increasing, oil pipelines such as those that follow the Rhine from Rotterdam and from the south could inflict serious, if accidental, damage, and projected power stations could raise the river's temperature to 35°C by 1985.

A Federal water management law was passed in 1957 setting out a general framework for water laws at *Länder* level and NRW enacted its own *Landeswassergesetz* in 1962, and has followed this by an active conservation programme. The *Land* Development Programme laid particular emphasis on the extension of mechanical-biological purification methods (between 1950 and 1970 the number of sewage plants doubled to over 900; 14 major plants and 300 minor ones were due for completion between 1970 and 1975), and on reducing pollution of the Rhine, Wupper, and

Ruhr in particular. Since 56 per cent of the area, 75 per cent of the population, and most of the industry of NRW is linked to Rhine drainage, this emphasis is only reasonable.

Recreation and countryside conservation

Pressure on space and changes in land-use are processes implicit in much of the foregoing discussion, and NRW, like most industrial regions, is faced by remorseless conversion of land from rural to urban use. In a society characterized by increasing mobility and leisure, the provision of open spaces and recreational areas demands high priority action. As such, the problem may be divided into two principal categories apart from the more general attempts through legislation to promote conservation and landscape protection: local recreational facilities —*Tageserholung*—provide easily accessible sites for day to day use, whereas *Wochenend und Ferienerholung* sites involve more distant recreational facilities for weekend and holiday movements. Few Germans own their own houses, rents are high, and with the preponderance of flats, open-air facilities are vital.

Much of NRW comprises areas of outstanding natural beauty, particularly in the uplands, and the existence of famous health spas and holiday centres (including skiing resorts) is a feature of the Sauerland and Weserbergland. Considerable investment is, however, being made under the 1970–5 Development Programme to improve tourist and weekend facilities in about thirty new centres, and reservoir environs such as those of the Rursee and Biggetalsperre offer important growth points. So too, extensive forested uplands provide an ideal outlet for the industrial population, and NRW has a substantial share of Germany's designated 'nature parks' and 'landscape protection areas' falling under Federal or State authority (Figs. 1 and 8). With, for example, 11 of the 40 *Naturparke*, NRW's population is well served in areas ranging from the Nordeifel (1355 km²) to the Siebengebirge (42 km²) near Bonn, and these are supplemented by a special category of eight similar *Bevorzugte Erholungsgebiete* totalling a further 10 000 km².

But much of the emphasis is on areas within, or easily accessible to, the built-up areas, in terms both of specific facilities and of more general improvement of the environment. The Ruhr furnishes the best examples of both *Tageserholung* and reclamation, and the reasons for this response are self-evident in the figures in Table 17 on changing land-use, in an area of

The Bigge reservoir in the Sauerland. Built between 1950 and 1965, the reservoir has a capacity of 150 million m³. The town of Attendorn is beside the far shore

4590 km², particularly the erosion of rural categories by urban uses.

Recreational areas fall into three categories, the first two being planned on a regional basis, the third by local authorities: recreation centres, e.g. Essen's Lake Baldeney, cover about 300 ha; recreation parks (*Revierparks*) range between 25 and 35 ha, and two of the three so far planned are now complete at Gysenberg, near Herne and at Nienhausen near Gelsenkirchen; urban leisure facilities (around 10 ha) are more numerous and dispersed.

The changing attitudes towards environment are best seen in general landscaping and reclamation undertaken by the Ruhr Planning Authority. Perhaps the most far-sighted development has been the creation of a regional open spaces system, which is establishing a series of six north-to-south green belts and preventing further coalescence of the Ruhr agglomeration. Between 1952 and 1971 some 1600 ha of 'new' countryside, largely linked with these belts, was created by reclamation of derelict land (including 500 ha of mining tips) and over the same period the Authority completed 1135 separate conservation projects, including 212 connected with public open spaces and 178 with landscaping involving such technical installations as power stations and sewage plants.

The case of the Rhenish Brown Coalfield

As an example of conservation in practice, particularly in its organizational and ecological aspects, it would be hard to find a better example than the *Braunkohlenrevier*. Open-cast mining of lignite has continued in the area west of the

TABLE 17

Land-use change in the Ruhr Planning Area: 1893–72
(percentage of total surface area)

Category	1893	1960	1972
Agriculture	67·5	56·1	51·3
Woodland	20·3	15·0	15·9
Wasteland	3·9	2·9	2·5
Lakes, rivers, and canals	1·4	2·2	2·4
Built-up areas	3·1	14·9	16·6
Traffic and transport	3·4	7·1	8·5
Urban open space (including recreation areas)	0·4	1·8	2·8

Rhine since 1766, although the modern, highly mechanized era dates only from around 1877 when briquettes became important. The area concerned is one of 3000 km² in the triangle between Köln, Neuss, and Düren (Fig. 2), with a geology in which Tertiary lignite seams, varying in thickness from 20 to 105 metres, lie as a series of gently dipping, block-faulted measures, protected from erosion by an overburden of gravel, sand, and loess. Three main deposits are distinguished (Fig. 10): those of the Ville Ridge, which, because they are as little as 20 m below the surface, were first to be commercially exploited; those of the southern coalfield which includes Eschweiler and Jülich, which are as much as 200 m below the surface; and finally those of the main coalfield between the Erft and Rur rivers which lie even deeper.

Brown coal is exploited principally as the cheapest source of energy, and the coalfield produces about 20 per cent of the Federal German Republic's electricity from an installed capacity in 1971 of 7800 MW, planned to increase to 11 500 MW by about 1976. In addition the lignite continues to be an important domestic fuel in briquette form. Production of brown coal is currently about 90 million tonnes (equivalent in energy to 28 million tonnes of hard coal), having risen from 5 million tonnes in 1900. Reserves total at least 55 billion tonnes although many seams are inaccessible with present open-cast techniques. The year 1955 was a turning point in that it marked the introduction of the first large bucket wheel excavator, a machine of 7400 tonnes capable of extracting 100 000 m³ daily; by 1975 a machine with double this capacity, capable of filling a 210 km-long goods train each day, will be in operation. Such a revolutionary machine depends, however, on an intricate system of conveyor belts feeding direct to the power stations, together with a highly organized railway network of 522 km operated by the company concerned (*Rheinbraun*). Only 16 000 workers are employed in the mines and associated workshops and briquette factories, together with another 16 000 in the power stations, and the number of working collieries has fallen from 23 in 1950 to 7 in 1971. The visual impact of open-cast mining, no less than the industry's

Fig. 10. The Rhenish Brown coalfield

Source: Rheinische Braunkohlenwerk A.G. 1971

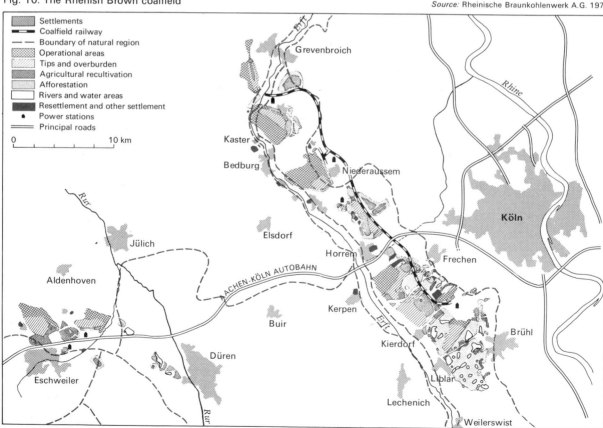

problems, has increased to match the scale of such operations.

Where the older mines had involved the stripping of overburden from coal in the ratio of 0·3 to 1, the ratio now rises to between 3 and 6 to 1. This overburden, in part loess and loessial loam—albeit often sour because of leaching—is necessarily removed during mining, and a total of up to 200 million tonnes of waste material is available each year. Much of the spoil and topsoil is transported by rail as far as 50 km south to old pits where reserves were exhausted in 1960, or experimentally over shorter distances by pipeline, as part of the systematic reclamation of abandoned workings. Present open-cast working has attained depths of up to 280 m and figures of well over 300 m are in prospect. Such operations are increasingly demanding comprehensive planning up to twenty years ahead. This involves not only detailed survey, the purchase and resettlement of farms and villages, and the provision of a technical infrastructure, but also what has been termed 'creative landscape conservation' prompted in part by specific legislation enacted in 1950, which obliges industry to participate actively in reclamation.

Broadly the new man-made landscape is either one of reclaimed agricultural land or of forest-lake landscape (Fig. 11). Current reclamation affects about 300 ha of farmland and 200 ha of forest each year, a rate of rehabilitation which has exceeded mining inroads since 1965. By 1971, of the 15 000 ha used up by brown coal mining since its inception, no less than 8207 ha (2992 ha of farmland and 4167 ha of forestry, excluding lakes) had been reclaimed, and in the twenty years up to 1971, 3300 farm holdings and 15 main settlements had been resettled. Yet in some senses the cultural landscape poses fewer problems than the physical landscape, in that mining has wrought not only edaphic but also hydrological and microclimatic modifications which make the establishment of new plant communities particularly difficult. In ecological terms the abandoned pits are case studies of rapidly changing landscapes and plant successions. Since 1958 much of the earlier reclamation pattern of single species afforestation has been replaced by a more balanced ecosystem. The recreational potential of the forest-lake landscapes is obvious, and recreation areas are important in the shallower abandoned workings of the southern Ville (Fig. 11).

A less obvious but crucial problem of the industry, which is likely to be turned to unexpected advantage, is the disturbance of the

Rheinisch–Westfälisches Elektrizitäswerk AG

A bucket-wheel excavator capable of extracting 100 000 m³ of overburden or brown coal a day

hydrology: an estimated 17 m³ of groundwater is removed for every ton of lignite mined, and this constitutes about 1·3 million million m³ annually. Some 900 pumps remove this water to the rivers Erft, Inde, and Merzbach, or to the 22 km-long *Kölner Randkanal*, specially built for drainage to the Rhine. With the prospect of water shortage in NRW, plans are now being discussed which may lead to the conversion of the deeper workings to reservoirs at a cost of DM 0·10 per m³, a fiftieth of conventional upland reservoir costs. Some 155 million m³ is currently supplied to local water boards, but this figure would be dwarfed if Rhine water were to be diverted via a tunnel to two proposed sites—the one at Garsdorf south of Grevenbroich (700 million m³ capacity), the other at Hambach north-west of Düren (2500 million m³).

The Rhenish Brown Coalfield epitomizes many of the contemporary problems discussed elsewhere, not least those attributable to the unprecedented effect of man (or his machines) on the landscape. Where deep mining hides most of the evidence from view—notwithstanding subsidence and spoil heaps—open-cast working has led to the devising of technical, social, and ecological solutions to the destructive occupation of the earth which arguably improve on what existed before.

Reg. Präs. Düsseldorf, No.18/20/296 ; Rheinisch-Westfälisches Elektrizitätswerk AG

The Heide Bergsee, the landscape of reclamation in the Rhenish Brown Coalfield

Fig. 11. Landscape ecology in the southern Ville before and after mining

Source: H. J. Bauer, 1963

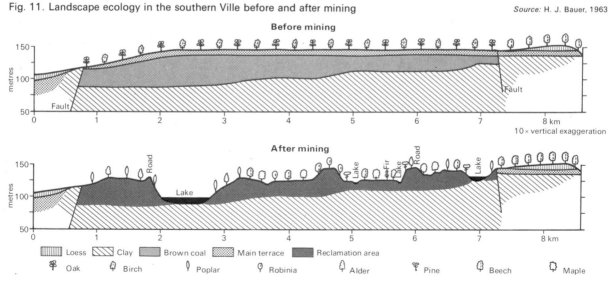

42

4 Planning for the Future

So far the picture has emerged of NRW as more a region with assorted problems than as a problem region in the accepted English sense with its overtones of depression or dereliction. Yet in terms of the future of its landscape and inhabitants it assuredly qualifies as a problem region in the political and administrative sense because solutions to its problems are increasingly being articulated on a regional basis. The German word *Raumordnung*, literally 'spatial ordering', comes closer than 'regional planning' in conveying the essentially holistic approach implicit in organizing space to give an optimum environment. Such spatial ordering is therefore more a philosophical than a scientific question, more a matter of practical politics than a theoretically-inclined *dirigisme*.

Although in Germany the *Wirtschaftswunder* has apparently eliminated 'depressed areas' along with unemployment and poverty, planning for the future has itself become something of a growth industry, and the face of NRW promises to undergo continuing change to eliminate potential structural weakness or imbalance. Even in conditions of high economic growth the phenomenon of regional disparity seems inevitable, and intervention by government bodies is necessary if the social, economic, and cultural well-being of the population is to be maintained at uniform levels.

This chapter will examine certain aspects of plans and planning in NRW in an endeavour to return to a synoptic view of the region and also to raise certain questions linked with the aims and options open to those plotting the future course of a territorial and social complex finding itself in the forefront of change. NRW deserves to be investigated as a regional planning model in which familiar and less familiar theories are being put into practice, a place where one prototype of 'the future' is being worked out.

NRW and the Federal system

Much of the interest in Government participation in planning—whether local or national—stems from the inherent difficulties in harmonizing the conceptual and legislative foundations from which policy is developed at E.E.C., Federal, or State level. Under the West German constitution the Government is required to provide similar living conditions for its citizens in all parts of the Federal territory, yet its functions are indicative and legislative rather than mandatory and executive. The *Länder* act as its agents, albeit with a high degree of autonomy, but it is the Federal Government in Bonn which represents them in international affairs. Such decentralization has great merits when contrasted with the metropolitan rigidities of Paris *vis-à-vis* its *départements* or the isolation of London from the 'provinces', but the obvious weakness of this constitutional arrangement is apparent in any attempt to plan Germany as a whole, rather than as the sum of its parts.

To write of 'planning' poses an immediate dilemma, for the Republic has adhered to a social market economy ill-disposed towards central planning in any form and strongly in contrast to the neo-collectivism of France for example. Such a policy implies a minimum of intervention on the assumption that the decisions and plans of individual producers and consumers are best co-ordinated by market mechanisms, which must in turn be preserved and stimulated by the Government. Adherence to the competitive order as a regulator of the economy has met with conspicuous success, judged by the economic strength of Germany, but many of the contemporary problems discussed earlier point to the need for detailed physical planning to be integrated within a regional planning framework. The national political shift from a Conservative–Liberal coalition Government to a Social-Democrat–Liberal one is not without significance in planning terms, and the NRW *Landesregierung* has, since 1946, had several coalition cabinets involving Social-Democrats in key ministries, culminating in *S.P.D.*-dominated coalitions since 1966.

After 1945 the Federal Government designated certain regions which lagged behind the general economic development as depressed areas (*Notstandsgebiete*) eligible for government aid; in NRW only the war-damaged agricultural zone of the western borders came into this category. In 1955 the depressed areas were restyled 'promotion areas' (*Fördergebiete*), but NRW stood out from most of the other *Länder* in having remarkably few areas judged to be 'unsound' enough to be incorporated into the 'Regional Action Programme'. The 1966–7 recession led to a new Federal programme in 1969, but by 1972 the only areas involved in the continuing programme were the northern Eifel-Aachen border area, south-east Westphalia and the west Münsterland with part of the northern Ruhr: these areas received Federal funds earmarked for the improvement of the existing infrastructure and for the promotion of trade and industry. (In national terms, however, 33 per cent of the population and 58 per cent of the area of Germany were involved in the 21 regional programmes running in 1973).

Probably more important for NRW have been the various planning laws enacted in Bonn to provide a legal framework for detailed proposals. It is important to note here that the German literature refers to three main areas of planning: *Städtebau* is concerned with town and country planning, *Landesplanung* with State planning by particular *Länder*, and *Raumordnung* with regional planning. Local authorities have full autonomy in their own areas over building control and other developments. This autonomy is vested in them by a Land Use and Development Control Act, but co-ordination between first, second and third tier authorities (local authority, Regional Planning Corporation or Association, and *Land* Planning Authority respectively) is obligatory.

The year 1911 marked the first move towards regional planning, but for modern NRW the setting up of the *Siedlungsverband Ruhrkohlenbezirk* or Ruhr Regional Planning Authority (hereafter *S.V.R.*) in 1920, was crucial. The principles of regional planning were first embodied in legislation enacted in 1933 and 1934, and in 1935 a Reich Office for National and Regional Planning was set up; the associated Acts remained in force under the new 1949 constitution. In 1960 the Federal Government passed an Act for Development Control, which laid down procedures to be followed at *Land* level, and in 1965 the Regional Planning Act (*Raumordnungsgesetz* or *ROG*), which has had far-reaching implications.

NRW's development plans

The first *Land* Planning Act (*Landesplanungsgesetz*) was passed in 1950, and apart from making the three Planning Corporations of the Rhineland, Westphalia-Lippe, and the Ruhr responsible for regional planning activities it recognized regional planning as a major function of the *Land*. This law was superseded in 1962 by the second *Landesplanungsgesetz* (subsequently revised again in 1972), which required the formulation of state and regional development programmes and marked the change from negative or reactive planning to positive or development planning. NRW promulgated its first *Land Development Programme* in August 1964, anticipating the *ROG* by nearly a year and making it the first German *Land* to produce a comprehensive set of planning tasks and objectives.

The Programme falls into two main parts. The first sets out the planning principles. Amongst these are sixteen specific principles, including determination to avoid or remedy excessive concentration, to preserve where possible agricultural and wooded areas, to encourage movement of new industries to 'economically weak areas', and to aim at 'the efficient co-ordination between dwellings and places of work'. NRW was divided into three Zones: the agglomeration cores (population density already or imminently in excess of 2000/km²), the agglomeration fringes (average 1000–2000/km²) and the rural zones (primarily exploited for agriculture or forestry). From this, three main planning tasks were derived, referring broadly to these three Zones. It stipulated regulation of areas in which undesirable development and spatial disorder is characteristic (*Ordnungsraum*), the safeguarding of areas where spatial order is threatened by unplanned development (*Sicherungs- und Gestaltungsräume*), and preparatory planning in Development Areas (*Förderungsräume*). This tripartite division can usefully be described as involving remedial, preventive or promotive policies.

The planning objectives thus set out in 1964 hinged on two key factors: first, the expected growth and zonal distribution of population, and, secondly, the concentration of settlement within a co-ordinated system of growth poles and axes.

Population increase

From a 1964 total of 16·4 million people in NRW it was expected that the population would pass 17·2 million by 1970, 18·5 million by 1980, and 20·5 million by 2000 A.D. On the basis of this trend, elaborate policies on manpower planning, social provision, and related matters were formulated. In the event this prognosis has needed substantial revision, largely because of the fall in birth-rate since 1965 (attributed to the '*Anti-baby Pille*') and a figure nearer 17·82 million is forecast for 1980. Such a shortfall of 700 000 people has obvious implications for the State, not least its

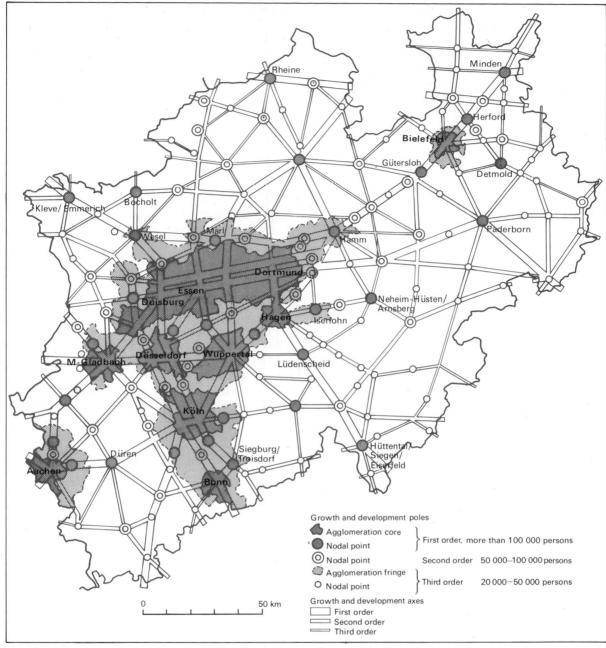

Fig. 12. NRW Development Plan – growth poles and axes

Source: NRW Government, 1970

TABLE 18

Area and population of the NRW Planning Zones

Zone	Area		Population 1970		Predicted growth 1964–80 millions
	km²	% NRW	millions	% NRW	
I. Agglomeration cores	2911	8·6	7·94	46·4	0·6
II. Agglomeration fringes	4565	13·4	3·43	20·0	0·5
III. Rural areas	26562	78·0	5·75	33·6	1·0

Source: Ministerialblatt 17, 1971.

increasing reliance on migrant workers. The actual population re-distribution in the three planning Zones, based on an increase of 2·5 million between 1964 and 1980, makes interesting reading and the shifts are summarized in Table 18 and Fig. 12.

Because of the urban congestion in Zone I only a limited population increase can be adequately housed. Two thirds of this increase is planned to be absorbed by the 'Rhine Line' towns between Krefeld, Düsseldorf, Köln, and Bonn; the Bergisches Land group of Wuppertal, Solingen, and Remscheid; plus Aachen and Mönchen Gladbach-Rheydt to the west of the Rhine. The Ruhr District will probably be capable of absorbing less than 200 000 more people.

Zone II broadly extends over the *Umland* of many of these cities, plus others like Bielefeld. About 50 per cent of the increase is expected to occur along the Rhine or near Aachen, 40 per cent in the *S.V.R.* area and only 10 per cent in Westphalia.

Zone III accounts for nearly four fifths of NRW and will absorb a planned million people by 1980. New settlement will gravitate towards small and medium-sized towns, which will be deliberately developed as central places.

Growth poles and axes

The second key feature in the 1964 *Land* Development Plan was a system of growth poles and axes, into which the overall development of the *Land* was to be directed. Fig. 12 illustrates both the tripartite zonation (communal infrastructure) and this framework (band infrastructure). It will be immediately apparent that such a model tends to accentuate the development of 'agglomeration bands' or linear cities while dividing the rural areas into inconveniently-shaped residuals. This schematic plan has legal standing, having been signed by the NRW Minister President in amended form in 1970. It is a rationalization of the now well known phenomenon of a central place hierarchy and a recognition that a Government has the power to re-distribute the forces involved in such functional regionalization.

Accordingly the Federal and the *Länder* Governments have prepared lists of designated central places and their dependent areas, and in the case of NRW all the more important settlements fall into four categories, recognized by the German *Raumordnungs* Conference since 1968: namely, *Kleinzentren* (elementary develop-

ment centres), *Unterzentren* (small urban centres or sub-centres with a population between 10 000 and 20 000 in their dependent areas), *Mittelzentren* (medium urban centres: 20 000–100 000), and *Oberzentren* (major urban centres: 100 000 and over). Since the two highest levels 'have been determined by history', regional planners have the particular task of artificially developing the two lower grades where necessary. In NRW this task is reflected in the designation of three orders of development poles or centres having central-place importance for a dependent area of at least 20 000 to 50 000 and upwards. First-order centres (excluding the agglomeration cores) total thirty places, ranging from Kleve-Emmerich and Düren to Rheine, Minden, and Siegen. An intermediate second-order (50 000–100 000) encompasses 45 regional centres, and the third-order (20 000–50 000) includes another 70 regional centres in the rural zone.

Linked with these central places is the network of first-, second- and third-order growth or development axes (Fig. 12), which reflect the provision and concentration of transportation media and public utilities. Thus the first-order axes link first-order central places, and must possess at least multi-track electrified railways, long-distance roads of motorway standard, water and power supply sufficient for industry, and sewage treatment provision. Second-order axes are those not developed to the higher standard, but regarded as of major importance for future development of the *Land*, whilst third-order axes provide the essential linkages to complete the system.

The NRW Programme 1975

It is one thing theoretically to plan for an elegant economic landscape and utopian society, but quite another to put the strategy into effect. The *Land* Development Plans I & II (Fig. 12) present as it were the bird's eye view of the future infrastructure, but at ground level very much data collection remains to be done before detailed planning proposals can be formulated for all the *Kreise*. Such proposals for action are intermittently appearing as specialized documents and general indications of the shape of things to come must be sought in two particular documents. The *Entwicklungsprogramm Ruhr* appeared in 1968, following on the promulgation of the first legally-binding Regional Development Plan for the Ruhr by the *S.V.R.* two years earlier. Many of its proposals for action have already been discussed, and followed from the Ruhr's peculiar economic crisis. Probably the most important single change arising from the programme is the linking of major settlements by a rapid transport system, already described in the case of Gelsenkirchen, which will transform the pattern of commuting and laboursheds.

In 1970 the second medium-term 'Plan for Action' (*Handlungsplan*) was published by the Düsseldorf government for the whole *Land*—the 'NRW Programme 1975'. Its theme was planned change and the investment priorities were determined by the need to ensure NRW's continued viability and prosperity. Expenditure for the seven sectors is summarized in Table 19.

TABLE 19
Expenditure in NRW, 1970

Sector	Investment (million DM)
Economy and Labour	2 896
Education & Research	9 917
Planning, Construction, Transport	12 862
Leisure and Culture	1 031
Health and Social Services	2 282
Water, Refuse, Pollution Control	1 168
Government and Administration	985
Total	31 141

The figures of Table 19 alone, show how far-reaching is the attempt at re-structuring the economy and society; how much the future prosperity is judged to depend on raising educational levels and ensuring a workforce capable of employment flexibility; how much emphasis on recreation and conservation is linked with planning the modern industrial state; how important is accessibility to high-speed communications networks for the society of the future. The plan demonstrates the degree to which modern technology is being used to eliminate sub-regional disparities, and emphasises how far the modern state is moving away from parochialism and isolation towards an almost wholly urbanized homogeneous society. The abandonment of traditional administrative frameworks is proceeding fast with the *Neugliederung*, or local government reform both territorial and functional, which underlies the complete reorganization of governmental space.

Problems remain, and not least those associated with a Republic which may ultimately contain only five *Länder*, including a renamed Rheinland-Westfalen. But even more important are the long-term implications of E.E.C. decisions, particularly those on social, regional, and transport policy. The NRW Programme came appropriately at the end of the first 25 testing years of the *Land*'s existence, a period marked by rehabilitation and consolidation. Undoubtedly, if the Treaty of Rome remains in operation, the next 25 years will be marked by the problems of harmonization and Europeanization.

Further Work

Although most of the literature on NRW is in German, it would be unfortunate if the language problem were to deter readers from following up particular themes partially developed in this book. Even without a working knowledge of German, much can be gained from the prolific cartographic and statistical sources in order to supplement such well-known texts as R. E. Dickinson's *Germany, A Regional and Economic Geography* (Methuen 1961) or T. H. Elkins' *Germany* (Chatto & Windus 1968) and to provide a solid base for detailed fieldwork. Probably the best introduction for the regional geographer is the *Topographischer Atlas Nordrhein-Westfalen* (Landesvermessungsamt NRW: Düsseldorf 1968) and the *Luftbildatlas Nordrhein-Westfalen* by U. Muuss and A. Schüttler (Karl Wachholtz Verlag, Neumünster 1969). The former contains 138 topographic sheet sections at varying scales, arranged by natural region and the latter compliments the map volume with some 80 oblique air photographs in colour in a similar format.

Comprehensive statistics for NRW are readily accessible in the compact annual *Statistisches Jahrbuch NRW*, and most Government departments, industries, and city administrations publish annual reports intended for the non-specialist. *German International* (Heinz Möller Verlag, Bonn), a monthly periodical in English, is a particularly up-to-date source on economic, social and political developments.

For those who read German the best source on current research in NRW is contained in the *Berichte zur deutschen Landeskunde* bibliographies. Local geographical research is included in certain university research monograph series, among them the *Arbeiten zur rheinischen Landeskunde* (Bonn), *Spieker* (Münster), the *Kölner geographische Arbeiten* and the *Bochumer geographische Arbeiten* (Bochum), and on occasion in journals such as *Erdkunde*, *Geographische Rundschau* and *Zeitschrift für Wirtschaftsgeographie*. Outside the universities there are many other research publications relevant to NRW's problems, such as the *S.V.R.*'s *Schriftenreihe*, the coal industry's *Glückauf* and the iron and steel industry's *Stahl und Eisen*. Although it is assumed that reference will be made to standard topographic maps (particularly at the 1:50 000 and the 1:200 000 scales), a useful supplement

for detailed local studies is the series of low-cost German school atlases published by the List Verlag for many individual cities or city regions; the NRW Planning Atlas and the *S.V.R.*'s *Regionalplanung* (atlas) are important sources.

For those able to undertake an excursion in the region, NRW offers a dense coverage of youth hostels, numerous museums (particularly the local Heimatmuseen), and a tradition amongst industrial firms of providing educational visits.

Of the many museums the following are particularly recommended in terms of themes developed in the book:
Museum of Industry and Commerce (Land Museum) in Düsseldorf.
Mining Museum (Bergbau Museum) in Bochum.
Information Centre (Brown Coal) at Schloss Paffendorf (near Bergheim).
Rhineland Regional Museum in Bonn.
Rhenish Open Air Museum at Kommern/Eifel, and other similar museums at Hagen and Detmold.

Selected further reading

Barr, J., 'Planning for the Ruhr', *Geographical Magazine* **42** (1970) 280–9.
Bauer H. J., 'Recultivation in the lignite mining areas of the Rhineland', *Geoforum* **8** (1971), 31–41.
Blacksell, A.M.Y., 'Recent changes in the morphology of West German townscapes' in *Urbanization and its problems*, edited by R. P. Beckinsale & J. M. Houston (Blackwell 1968) 199–217.
Dickinson, R. E., 'The geography of commuting in Western Germany', *Annals of the Association of American Geographers* **49** (1959) 443–56.
Elkins, T. H., 'The Cologne Brown Coal Field', *Transactions of the Institute of British Geographers* **19** (1953), 131–43.
Hall, P., *The World Cities* (Weidenfeld & Nicolson, 1966) 122–57.
Holzner, L., 'The role of history and tradition in the urban geography of West Germany', *Annals of the Association of American Geographers* **60** (1970), 315–39.
Mayhew, A., *Rural settlement and farming in Germany* (Batsford, 1973).
Pounds, N. J. G., *The Ruhr. A Study in Historical and Economic Geography* (Faber & Faber 1952).
Rugg, D., 'Selected areal effects of planning processes upon urban development in the Federal Republic of Germany', *Economic Geography* **42** (1966) 326–35.
Wiel, P. *Wirtschaftsgeschichte des Ruhrgebietes* (*S.V.R.* 1970).